D1433291

PRAISE FOR *RARE LEADERSHIP IN THE WORKPLACE*

The bedrock of leadership is being the right kind of person, not simply the person with the right ideas. Without a cultivated core, leaders will not mature with their responsibilities and opportunities to serve. *Rare Leadership in the Workplace* guides leaders through the critical rooted growth that enables them to lead their teams to new heights.

Roger Parrott
President of Belhaven University and author of *The Longview: Lasting Strategies for Rising Leaders*

I loved *Rare Leadership in the Workplace*! Marcus and Jim make a compelling, scientifically verified case that the key to mature, effective leadership is "the high-powered fuel of joy." This book will convince you of that truth and provide a practical roadmap to returning to joy each day so you can do your most exceptional work.

Jordan Raynor
National bestselling author of *Called to Create* and *Master of One*

Just about every book on leadership relives the same worn message—inspire, motivate, be a visionary, get great results. *Rare Leadership in the Workplace* is that one leadership book in a thousand you should actually read and apply.

Chuck Blakeman
Author of *Making Money Is Killing Your Business*

As a business owner and CEO, I learned long ago my business exists for more than profit. It must be a force for good in the world around us. *Rare Leadership in the Workplace* by Marcus Warner and Jim Wilder adds brain science to the fundamental leadership principles that instruct us to seek true success—contentment with joy.

Martin Ozinga III
Chairman, Ozinga

In *Rare Leadership in the Workplace*, we get some simple yet profound answers. In my blue-collar world, I need practical concepts I can personally implement and teach to my staff. This book is possibly the most concise and relevant book on leadership I have ever read. It doesn't bog down the reader with theory but helps us tap into the deep reality that mature leaders create effective work cultures and that joy is a powerful force in the workplace.

Dave Hataj

Author of *Good Work*; president and owner of Edgerton Gear, Inc.

Jim Wilder is an unsung hero with remarkably powerful concepts that are truly life-changing. *Rare Leadership in the Workplace* is an absolute must-read for business leaders who strive for uncommon impact in their world. This book is an instruction manual on doing life differently a s a business leader from a truth-focused point of view. The RARE habits are incredibly applicable throughout countless facets of life, and in the workplace, these habits will carry you to extraordinary success!

Jeff Reeter

Entrepreneur, business leader, speaker, author

Rare Leadership in the Workplace, written as a primer that is both practical and profound, is full of ideas that will revitalize a leader's style, recommit them to the desire to innovate, and finally release them to constantly evaluate. Offered in a pull-push format, the approach offered by Warner and Wilder is partly qualitative and partly quantitative. Its formulaic approach is easy to adapt and more importantly encouraging to adopt. It truly is a refreshing and timely offering that will strengthen the leadership toolbox of individuals and institutions.

Krish Dhanam

Former Vice President of Ziglar Worldwide; CEO of Skylife Success; coauthor of *Hardheaded & Softhearted* (with the former president of Microsoft)

Marcus Warner / Jim Wilder

Rare
Leadership

IN THE WORKPLACE

4 Uncommon Habits That Improve
Focus, Engagement, and Productivity

NORTHFIELD PUBLISHING

CHICAGO

Some content in this book was adapted from content previously published on lifemodel.org.

Edited by Elizabeth Cody Newenhuyse
Interior design: Puckett Smartt
Cover design: Erik M. Peterson
Cover image of trees copyright © by ykononova/Shutterstock (254219002). All rights reserved.
Jim Wilder photo: Christopher Kamman

Library of Congress Cataloging-in-Publication Data

Names: Wilder, Jim, author. | Warner, Marcus, author.
Title: Rare leadership in the workplace : four habits that improve focus, engagement, and productivity / Jim Wilder, Marcus Warner.
Description: Chicago : Northfield Publishing, [2021] | Includes bibliographical references. | Summary: "Combining theology, cutting-edge brain science, and decades of counseling and consulting experience, Rare Leadership shows you how to take your leadership and team to the next level. Whether you are burnt out or just looking to improve, it will revive your leadership and equip you to lead healthy, happy, and effective teams"-- Provided by publisher.
Identifiers: LCCN 2020053384 (print) | LCCN 2020053385 (ebook) | ISBN 9780802421906 (paperback) | ISBN 9780802499318 (ebook)
Subjects: LCSH: Leadership. | Organizational behavior.
Classification: LCC HD57.7 .W5237 2021 (print) | LCC HD57.7 (ebook) | DDC
  658.4/092--dc23
LC record available at https://lccn.loc.gov/2020053384
LC ebook record available at https://lccn.loc.gov/2020053385

We hope you enjoy this book from Northfield Publishing. Our goal is to provide high-quality, thought-provoking books and products that connect truth to your real needs and challenges. For more information on other books and products that will help you with all your important relationships, go to northfieldpublishing .com or write to:

Northfield Publishing
820 N. LaSalle Boulevard
Chicago, IL 60610

3 5 7 9 10 8 6 4 2

Printed in the United States of America

Contents

Introduction

WHAT SEPARATES THE LEADERS we love to follow from those we have to follow? The answer comes down to one word: maturity. We love following leaders who handle themselves like adults. At best we tolerate leaders who are immature, because they add trouble to the problems we already face.

The best leaders are not just visionaries, they are mature people. They handle relationships and tasks with excellence. There is a secret to this type of maturity. These people have learned how to run their lives on the high-octane fuel of joy. That may be surprising to you. There aren't a lot of leadership books citing joy as the key to success. But relational joy is crucial to leadership effectiveness. When leaders recognize that joy is not simply the icing on the cake of a good day, but the fuel that drives what they do, it can sustain them through the hard issues and the weight that comes with leadership.

Motivation is all about emotion. Leaders who constantly motivate themselves and their team with negatives like fear, anger, and shame will not thrive for long. Leaders who learn to love the people they are working with, handle their emotions with competence, and keep themselves and others inspired by what brings joy become leaders we love to follow.

In this book we want to help you become a more effective leader. What makes a leader effective are the accumulated skills and habits we use without ever thinking about them. When you develop the skills and habits related to maturity, they become a part of you and start showing up automatically which greatly increases your effectiveness.

You can grow both your ability to live with joy and your ability to lead with maturity, and we want to help. These two goals are actually inseparable. Mature people handle the hardships of life well because they know how to remain relational under stress, act like themselves when problems arise, and return to joy after their emotions get triggered. None of this is possible without learning skills and building habits that increase your ability to run on the fuel of joy.

We (Jim and Marcus) have been friends for fifteen years. I (Jim) have been working in brain science research for thirty years. During this time my team at the counseling center I led in Southern California developed an idealized model of what is supposed to happen at each stage of maturity development. It is called the Life Model and is based on research coming out of the UCLA Medical Center and the work of brain science experts like Allan Schore and Daniel Siegel, Iain McGilchrist, and others. The model our team developed has proven highly effective in dealing with some of the most difficult clinical issues on the planet.[1]

In working on this book, we have taken the Life Model and applied it to the challenges of leadership. We want to help you learn how to grow maturity and live with greater joy. At the heart of our approach are four habits that characterize the mature leaders people love to follow.

We first published on this topic five years ago. Since then we have had many opportunities to teach these principles in businesses and nonprofits with great response. We hope this becomes a book you refer to again and again and pass on to others. If we do our job right, you will find this to be the kind of book that will transform not only your leadership, but your whole approach to life.

MARCUS WARNER
Carmel, Indiana

JIM WILDER
Evergreen, Colorado

Note: Many names and stories in this book have been altered slightly to protect the identities of the people involved. However, the stories accurately reflect the spirit of the events we report.

CHAPTER ONE

Leaders We Love to Follow

ONE OF THE FIRST GROUPS who invited me (Marcus) to teach on Rare Leadership didn't seem to realize what they had signed up for. As I waited for my opportunity to explain the habits of mature leaders to them, the owner of the company laid out a vision for his team. He opened with the unforgettable line: "We want to be ----- pirates!" That got my attention. I wondered where he was going with this. He continued, "We want our competitors to see our name on the bid sheet and say, 'Oh no, it's them! Those cutthroats will do whatever it takes to get this bid.'" He then wrapped up his introduction and said, "Now, here's Marcus to teach us about rare leadership."

I was a bit stunned. Someone clearly hadn't told him that rare leadership was about relational and emotional maturity. He didn't seem to see the difference between mature leadership and "do-whatever-it-takes" business ethics.

To this man's credit, he quickly got on board. Partway through our opening presentation, he realized that he wasn't very mature in the way he ran his company—or his family. At one point, after seeing a slide outlining the difference between mature people who live with their relational brain circuits on and immature people who live with them off, he blurted out, "I don't think I've ever had my relational circuits on." The rest of the people in the room all looked at me as if to say, "He's not lying."

After that moment, the questions started coming with great earnestness and, by the end of the meeting, his team signed up for a year of coaching on Rare Leadership with our lead trainer. The next year I was invited back to address the company's national management team. This time, instead of his "cutthroat" speech, the owner said, "We want to be a company that handles ourselves like adults. We want everyone we interact with to say, 'We love working with this company because we love the way they go about their business.' Now here's Marcus to teach us how to be mature leaders." I couldn't help but smile. He had come a long way.

Later that year, the CEO of this company told me he had started teaching the RARE model whenever he was asked to speak at leadership events. "Not only has it changed our culture," he told me, "it has improved our bottom line."

WE NEED MORE MATURE LEADERS

The lack of maturity in most leadership settings is becoming increasingly obvious. Psychologist and leadership expert Richard Davis wrote an article for the *Harvard Business Review* with the simple title, "We Need More Mature Leaders."[1] In this article he launches an attack on "sandbox leaders"—people who don't play well together. The childish behavior and narcissistic outlooks of these immature leaders place personal pride above the good of their organization. In summary, Davis writes:

> The timing could not be worse. The nation's current problems, as vast and overwhelming as they are, appear secondary to the whims of spoiled children, unwilling to play well together. At a time when we need solid, grounded leadership more than ever, we seem to be in short supply of adults who act like, well . . . like adults.[2]

I often show this quote on a slide when I teach at leadership events, and generally see heads nodding in agreement all across the room. Most assume the critique was ripped out of the current headlines and describes the mess we are in today. But I like to draw their attention to the fact that the article was written in 2011. That was quite a few years ago. It is a reminder that the level of maturity in this culture is not moving in the right direction. On the contrary, we are in the midst of a maturity crisis—not only in leadership but at all levels of society. If you have any doubt, just browse social media for a few minutes.

The purpose of this book is not to condemn or criticize anyone specifically. Rather, it is to call all of us to "up our game" when it comes to handling life with maturity. Mature leaders excel at building healthy cultures, solving problems relationally, and keeping relationships bigger than problems.

"SUPER CHICKENS": MATURITY VS. RESULTS

Sandbox leadership is a growing problem around the world. Most organizations are so results-driven, they don't put enough emphasis on the maturity of the people they hire and promote. Most leaders get where they are because they are good at solving problems and getting results. These attributes, however, have nothing to do with character or relational competence. The problem with hiring or promoting people strictly on the basis of results is that we often place selfish and immature individuals into important positions. Any short-term results come at the price of a toxic work culture. Our long-term results will not be what we hoped.

In a widely viewed TED talk, Margaret Heffernan argues that there is a serious flaw with only looking at results when evaluating performance. In her presentation, she tells about a researcher at Purdue University who conducted a simple experiment to measure egg production in chickens. The goal was improved production. They started with one group of chickens and counted how many eggs each one produced. Then they took the "top producers" (the ones who got the best results) and put them into a special group. They did this for six generations, hoping to breed a group of "super chickens" who would lay more eggs than "normal chickens." The results of the experiment were a bit shocking. Over six generations, the normal chickens saw their egg-production per chicken increase dramatically. When they measured results among the "super chickens," they found that only three of them were still alive! This was certainly not the conclusion they were expecting! It turned out that these were not super chickens at all but "predator chickens." They got better results than the rest because they pecked at the other chickens and kept their production low. When they were trapped in a group together, they literally pecked each other to death.[3]

This story must have something to do with life in corporate America, because Ms. Heffernan's TED talk has been watched by millions. For our purposes, it demonstrates the danger of emphasizing results over maturity in leadership. When results and maturity meet, you get the best of both worlds. The danger grows when results are elevated to the point that maturity no longer matters.

WHAT IS MATURITY?

Maturity is a collection of skills and habits we develop over time. Just like it takes hard work and repetition to build muscle, so it takes hard work and repetition to build maturity. And just as stronger muscles give you more capacity to handle weight, so greater maturity gives you more capacity to handle the hardships of life. From this perspective, maturity can be defined as enduring hardship well. The key word in that sentence is "well." We all suffer. We all endure hardship. What

> Mature people establish routines in their life that help them keep their joy levels high.

separates maturity from immaturity is the ability to suffer well. We will take a deeper dive into this idea in chapter 7, but here are a few thoughts to get us started.

Maturity requires joy. One of the keys to enduring hardship well is learning how to live life on the high-powered fuel of joy. Joy can be thought of as the air in the ball that lets it bounce. When you wake up feeling great and full of anticipation for the day ahead, you have lots of air in your ball. That joy makes it much easier to bounce back from the hard things that happen throughout the day. At the end of the evening we need a routine to help us replenish that joy so our tank is full for the next day. One of the characteristics of mature people is that they establish routines in their life that help them keep their joy levels high, so that they have the energy and emotional capacity to deal with the hard things that inevitably come their way.

So what do we mean by joy? It is surprising to many people to learn that from our brain's perspective, joy is always relational. Part of the joy of taking a walk and enjoying the fall colors or the golden hour of sunset is that it is a relational experience for us. It makes us feel connected to memories in the past of sharing such moments with people we loved. It makes us think of people with whom we would like to share the experience. Even the joy of finishing a project successfully is basically relational. We anticipate getting a "job well done" and a smile from someone who will be pleased with us and happy to see us.

The highest joy cultures in the world are the most relational. Take Denmark, for example. In study after study it ranks as one of the happiest cultures on earth.[4] But what's the secret? What do they do differently? In a nutshell, the Danish culture is anchored in a great rhythm of work, rest, and relationship. People often meet for coffee or beer after work, take time for strolls through the park, and have friends over for dinner in the evening. It is common for relational experiences like these to happen at some point every day. In addition, most Sundays are highlighted by a meal shared by extended family in which multiple generations of aunts, uncles, and cousins gather for food and fun. Having a life anchored in so much relational connection and joy creates a sense that you never go through anything alone. Relational joy provides security as well as energy for dealing with the ups and downs of life.

In stark contrast, American culture is highly individual. Families don't tend to stay together. We often hop from job to job and form very surface-level relationships. Without a relational anchor, we find it hard to replenish our joy and life becomes a grind. In the business world, leaders who learn how to build strong relational community in which people like working together and enjoy being around each other will have a much more engaged workforce.

Maturity requires a stable core identity. From a brain science perspective, maturity develops as we grow a relational sense of self that stays the same no matter what emotions we have to face. If I turn into a different person with every emotion I feel, I am functioning like an infant rather than an adult.[5]

Let's consider the case of Bob. Bob was a fun-loving person who was great at casting vision and getting people to join his cause. He was a gifted motivator, was driven by his vision, and developed a close circle of loyal friends. Bob loved to be the hero but didn't know how to handle being the problem. Over time, his friends began to notice that when Bob felt any shame or criticism, he often snapped at them and seemed to become a totally different person. Whenever something went wrong, Bob was known to stop the team meeting until someone took ownership for the failure. Bob himself never took ownership. One of his chief supporters gradually became Bob's whipping boy. Whenever something went wrong, this man often volunteered to take the blame, just to keep the meeting going. As long as Bob felt like you were on his side, he loved you like a brother. But if he sensed any opposition from you, he interpreted it as disloyalty, and Bob could be very harsh with disloyalty. Everyone liked Bob, the fun-loving visionary, but they were scared of Bob, the loyalty enforcer. They all learned to avoid subjects that brought out the enforcer. No one wanted to lift the lid on Pandora's box and unleash the chaos. It was safer just to keep Bob happy.

Few people understood that Bob had a maturity problem. Even fewer people recognized that Bob lacked skills related to handling shame. When Bob left and a new leader took his place, people suddenly felt like they could breathe more deeply. The entire atmosphere of the workplace changed. Only after they experienced the change did most people realize how toxic the environment had become.

When Bob felt shame, he flipped from friend mode into enemy mode. In an instant, he went from being someone you genuinely liked to someone scary. Bob could remain relational and act like himself a lot of the time, but when shame got triggered, it exposed a hole in his maturity. He stopped being relational and lost the ability to act like himself. Like an infant, he turned into a completely different person when he felt shame.

An inability to handle shame leads the Bobs of this world to instinctively justify themselves whenever a problem arises. They are experts at making sure that pain and blame get deflected to someone else. Instead of building the habits of mature leadership, they have built the habits of immature, sandbox leadership.

FOUR CORE HABITS OF MATURITY

Most of us can be relational and act like ourselves when life is easy. Maturity gets tested when life is hard. We have defined maturity as enduring hardship well. There is an inherent logic to this definition, especially when you think about the stages

> When Bob felt shame, he went from being someone you genuinely liked to someone scary.

of maturity development. You expect a child to handle hardship better than a baby. You expect a teen to handle suffering better than a child, and an adult to handle more stress than a teen. However, there is a difference between handling hardship and handling it well. The difference lies in a person's ability to remain relational, act like themselves, and return to joy in spite of the hardship. These are the four core habits of mature leaders. We will take a quick look at them now, explain the brain science behind them in the next chapter, and spend the rest of the book unpacking why these are so important and how to grow them.

The four habits of mature leaders can be remembered as a simple equation, summed up in the word RARE— R+A+R=E.

Remain relational
   plus
Act like yourself
   plus
Return to joy
   equals
Endure hardship well

Since mature leaders are often hard to find, the acrostic RARE seems appropriate.

Rare leaders often don't realize they have these four habits. They aren't simply choosing to do these things every time a problem arises. These habits show up automatically as part of their character. That is our goal. We want to practice skills until they become habits that show up without our having to think about them.

WHAT ARE THE MARKS OF AN EFFECTIVE LEADER?

Effective leaders are set apart by the maturity that shows up wherever they go. Their maturity serves as a catalyst for everything they do. It helps them focus on the right issues and make sure they are giving their conscious attention to the right things. It anchors their lives in habits that make them a welcome addition to any team. Their maturity also helps them excel at collaborative work. Unlike sandbox leaders who don't play well with others, one of the qualities that make mature leaders so effective is their high capacity for relational engagement. Maturity will always produce these three marks of effective leadership.

1. **Focus.** Effective leaders are good at focusing on tasks and decision-making that keep their teams and organizations moving forward. Focus is related to what gets our conscious attention (as opposed to what shows up automatically because it is part of our character and skill set). Focus is crucial to vision casting, problem solving, and getting work done. For some of us, that is all there is to

leadership, but really, focus is just the tip of the iceberg of all that goes into being an effective leader.

2. **Habits.** Effective leaders possess skills at deeper level than the ability to focus. These skills are related to our character, emotional capacity, relational competence, and all of the "soft skills" that are developed in a much deeper part of the brain than mere focus. Habits we have developed over time show up automatically wherever we go because they are formed in a part of the brain where activity can be thought of as "supraconscious." It is supraconscious as opposed to subconscious because it is happening in a part of the brain that processes activity faster than we can put things into words. We call this part of the brain the fast track.

Because these habits are formed in the part of our brain that operates faster than the speed of thought, they don't show up because we focus on them and choose to use them. They show up because we have taken the time to develop these skills so that they happen automatically. We see this in sports, music, and the arts. Most of what an athlete, musician, or artist does happens automatically. Their focus is not on the skills and habits they have already spent years developing. Their focus is on the mood, the creativity, and the situation at hand. If they have to stop and think about their technique or something else that is basic to the execution of their task, they are more likely to make mistakes than if they trust what they have learned and stay in the flow of the moment. In the same way that I don't stop to think about how to type as I (Marcus) write these words or I lose track of the flow of my words, effective leaders have habits and skills that have been developed in the supraconscious, superfast part of the brain. Any leader can practice focused attention. What separates mature leaders from sandbox leaders are the skill and habits they have developed that allow their character and relational skill to show up automatically.

3. **Collaboration.** The third mark of an effective leader relates to the ability to read the people around them and collaborate well. The ability to read situations correctly, calculate the timing and coordination of the preferred responses, and then direct the attention and energy of the people around the leader to work cooperatively affects a variety of leadership problems that need to be solved:

   - What will our customers need?
   - How will our team respond?
   - What value will our team provide effectively?
   - What will "synchronize" the team?
   - How will we reach our objectives?
   - What activities are sustainable for our team and our customers?

Most of this book will focus on the supraconscious skills and habits of mature leaders, but we wanted you to have a sense of how this all fits together. For those who like memory devices, you can remember these three essential elements of effective leadership as CASHCoW.

- Focus is CA—Conscious Attention
- Habits is SH—Supraconscious Habits
- Collaboration is CW—Collaborative Work

LIFTING THE LID

There is a difference between personal success and leadership effectiveness. I may succeed personally at tasks I undertake like finishing a project, preparing a report, or making a sale, but such successes are not the same as leading a team successfully. Many people who are good at getting work done individually lack the skills and habits to lead well. The lid on the effectiveness of most leaders is not a lack of task-related skills. It is also deeper than possessing "people skills." The real lid on leadership effectiveness is related to maturity skills. Put simply, immaturity sabotages leadership effectiveness; maturity grows it. Thus, if you want to become the sort of leader others love to follow, you need to grow your personal maturity skills. That is why we wrote this book. We want to help you begin building the four RARE habits that characterize mature leaders. In the process you will also learn how to increase trust and engagement in the people you lead.

One small business owner in the Portland area learned the four RARE habits and started teaching them to his team. He hung banners in his office and had signs placed on each desk that read, "Remain relational. Act like yourself. Return to joy. Endure hardship well." He put the signs next to the phones so that as his team members handled difficult calls and problematic emails, they had a constant reminder in front of them of how adults handle hardship. Within a month or two, these practices were starting to become habits. On one occasion when the manager was in his office complaining about a situation and struggling with his emotions, one of the team members—a person who had been notorious for their lack of grace—called out, "It sounds like someone needs to return to joy!" The manager laughed to himself and smiled broadly as he realized he was beginning to succeed in building a healthy culture with a common language to describe their values.[5] His people were even starting to remind him of how it was like them to act. By the team learning to handle hardship well, the maturity level in the office was growing.

I (Marcus) have some good friends who demonstrated rare leadership in the way they navigated the hardships caused by the pandemic in 2020. This husband-and-wife team run a business that employs nearly fifty people in a factory that refurbishes iron for a major railroad company. One of their top priorities was making sure that they kept running on the fuel of relational joy. They did this first by closely guarding time together in their marriage. They made sure they had an evening routine for winding down and relaxing together and that they put things on the calendar they could anticipate with excitement like date nights and short trips. They also dealt with their management team and employees in a way that collaboratively created solutions to the new problems they faced. They found ways to help their workers social distance and rotate shifts. They used the tax codes and government initiatives to maximum benefit, and actually raised salaries for their workers. Through it all, they acted like themselves. There were no meltdowns or shouting matches. They didn't avoid the problems but tackled them head-on. One of the reasons they were able to do this was that in prior years they had dismissed managers and workers whose immaturity had created a toxic environment, intentionally promoting those with greater maturity. As a result, they had a mature team in place when the crisis hit who were able to manage the hardship while remaining relational and acting like themselves.

The RARE habits of mature leaders demonstrated by these small business owners are anchored in an understanding of how the brain works. In the next chapter we will introduce a simple model of brain function that will help you understand how these habits work and why they are so important.

MATURITY WORKOUT: QUIETING

At the end of each chapter we will give you a recommended exercise you can start doing in order to begin growing your emotional capacity and thus your ability to handle hardship well. The first skill is quieting. In the book *Building Bounce*, which I (Marcus) wrote along with art therapist and child development expert Stefanie Hinman,[6] we recommend four BEST practices for quieting.

B—Breathing. Deep breathing is a good way to help your nervous system calm down from upset emotion. The Navy SEALs teach breathing in a box—inhale for a four-count, hold your breath for a four-count, exhale for a four-count, and hold for another four-count. You repeat this until you feel a bit more under control. In working with children, Stefanie often encourages them to "smell the soup" (inhale deeply), then blow on the soup (exhale fully). This is just another way of working on breathing. Take one to two minutes to breath in a box or smell and blow the soup, and see if you don't feel a little calmer.

E—Exaggerating. It rarely does any good to simply tell yourself (or someone else) to just calm down. It helps to exaggerate the emotion before quieting.

When you are angry, you might try (privately!) making a big angry face and clenching your fists, while blowing air out of your nose to make your nostrils flare. In this way you are exaggerating some of the physical elements of the anger you feel. After this, practice deep breathing and rubbing the tension out of your arms. You can do this three or four times if necessary. It can help you quiet yourself. You can do similar exercises with other emotions.

S—Soothing. Soothing can relate to your environment or your body. Building a fire in the fireplace, taking a hot shower or bath, sitting with heavy wool blankets, and rubbing your arms are just a few ways that people often take a few minutes or more to calm and quiet.

T—Tensing. Tensing and releasing muscle groups is another good quieting skill. You can do this on airplanes, in meetings, or at your desk. You simply focus on one set of muscles (arms, legs, shoulders) and tighten them for a count of five, then let the muscles relax. Exhaling deeply also helps.

Using these BEST practices when you feel tension rising can help you build the skills to quiet more quickly from upset emotions which is an important element of returning to joy.

CHAPTER 2

The Brain Science Behind Maturity

IN THIS CHAPTER, we will introduce three fundamental insights about the brain that help us understand what maturity is and how it is developed.

1. The brain craves the fuel of joy.
2. The brain has two very different operating systems.
3. The brain functions in levels.

These observations help us understand that maturity requires living with both operating systems of the brain functioning at peak capacity. Far too many of us live with one operating system mostly shut down and drive ourselves with fear rather than joy. When this happens it has a profoundly negative effect on our maturity levels, which can take a quick dive into the sandbox and diapers as soon as something goes wrong.

THE BRAIN CRAVES THE FUEL OF JOY

Your brain runs on one of two kinds of fuel: joy or fear. Joy is the natural fuel on which the brain wants to run. Fear is the second-rate alternative fuel on which it is often forced to run. For many of us, fear is the dominant fuel running our brain. We think in terms of damage control and live more to avoid what is overwhelming than to enjoy what is satisfying. Leaders who run on fear eventually burn out. They also burn out people they lead. Fear-driven leaders motivate themselves and others with the tools of fear: shame, anger, threats, and manipulation.

Whatever emotion we use to motivate ourselves will eventually become indispensable for motivating the people we lead. If we procrastinate because we need the surge of adrenaline that comes from the fear of missing a deadline, we will find ourselves using procrastination and the fear of deadlines to motivate our teams. If we yell at ourselves and call ourselves names when we need to get something done, guess what strategies we will turn to when we really need our team to get something done?

In stark contrast, leaders who learn to run on the fuel of joy find a sustainable source of motivation for themselves and others that never runs dry. This doesn't mean that you are happy all the time or that you never experience upsetting emotions (usually caused by upsetting people). Running on the fuel of joy means you find ways, every day, to build a little joy into the relationships you have.

Joy is the positive energy that comes from sharing a relational connection. If I have a good weekend camping with my friends, I can run for days on the emotional energy created by the joy we shared. If I am looking forward to a fun event with someone I love at the end of the week (a date with my spouse, a trip to the state park with my kids, a good book I can talk about with my best friend), that joy can give me the capacity I need to deal with a lot of garbage throughout the week. Beyond this, if I work on a high joy team, the relational energy helps all of us do our best, most creative work, and handle the challenges we face with a sense that we are in this together.

In the business world, joy may seem optional. It can feel like the bottom line of results is all that matters. But sustainable success and long-term satisfaction can only be found when there is relational joy involved in what we do. When we love being part of the team, when we appreciate each other's strengths and creative contributions, it creates a synergy that makes us smile and gives us energy. Effective leaders excel at building teams that form joy bonds rather than fear bonds. We will do anything for people we love. We will look for an exit strategy from people we fear.

As biological beings, joy is our normal state. We are relational creatures by nature. No one seeks treatment to reduce their joy levels. No one complains to coworkers about having too much joy in their lives. No one worries about loved ones who are "just too joyful these days." The problems happen

One of the primary tasks of leadership is the job of building a group around joy rather than fear.

when there is too little joy in our lives. When our lives get overwhelmed by problems and conflicts, we often forget that joy would be a natural and rewarding way to live. We don't even think of joy as something to pursue.

One of the primary tasks of leadership is the job of building a group around joy rather than fear. While many groups unite around a shared fear or problem, this is not a desirable long-term plan. Joy is our deepest motivation and need. Fear is always destructive as a long-term source of motivation.

THE BRAIN HAS TWO VERY DIFFERENT TRACKS

If you were able to look at your physical brain, you would see two halves that look exactly alike. The right and left hemispheres of the brain are mirrors of one another. However, these two hemispheres drive two completely different operating systems in your brain. We call them the fast track and the slow track.

The fast track is the operating system that regulates our emotions and helps us read what is going on in the world around us. It also remembers who we are and how it is like us to act. The part of the brain that thinks of itself as "me" is located on the fast track. As long as our fast track is operational and our relational circuits are running, we find it easier to stay engaged with life, live with joy, and act like ourselves.

The slow track is where we create narratives, solve problems, and perform tasks. The slow track calls up everything we know from the past in order to anticipate the future and try to create plans that will minimize damage. It is the verbal part of the brain where we do our thinking and decision making.[1]

Most leaders have well-developed slow tracks. They have been well trained to solve problems and get work done. However, they have not been well trained in the skills that make for a high-functioning fast track. What sets rare leaders apart from sandbox leaders is the fast track. Leaders who have great fast-track skills have the relational and emotional competence that makes us want to follow them.

SLOW TRACK VS. FAST TRACK

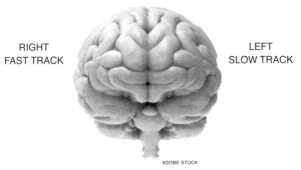

RIGHT
FAST TRACK

LEFT
SLOW TRACK

ADOBE STOCK

View from the front of the brain

YOUR BRAIN FUNCTIONS IN LEVELS

You can divide leadership brain functions into five levels. The first four are in the fast track. The fifth level is the slow track. If there is a problem at the lower levels, it will impact everything above it. All of the first four levels in the fast track should engage before we ever start thinking and strategizing about life.

These five levels can be thought of as an elevator that moves from one floor to the next. We call it the "joy elevator" because when it is working properly, our brains naturally run on the fuel of joy. But when the elevator gets stuck, fear creeps in and begins to take over. The first four levels of the joy elevator are sometimes called "the social engagement system" of the brain. Social intelligence controls what leaders do without having to think about it.[2] These four levels of the joy elevator form the control center of the brain as it interfaces with the world. Here is a brief description.

Attachment. The deepest level of brain integration is the attachment center, which is dominated by the thalamus and part of the basal ganglia called the nucleus accumbens (see diagram on p. 38). Our personal reality and attachment to people, substances, and experiences are created on the ground floor of the brain. The attachment level is sometimes called the "deep limbic system" and lights up when we want to bond with others. If we do not receive a response in return, we feel pained, rejected, unloved, abandoned, jilted, dumped, alone, or unwanted. The attachment level probably inspires more songs, stories, movies, relationships, and crimes than any other structure.

The desire for joyful attachment is the deepest craving of human experience. When something goes wrong with our attachments, we become dismissive or distracted, fearful, and potentially addicted. Problems at the attachment level affect all brain function above it. Notice what happens to a person's work and concentration when they are getting divorced or suffering a major loss. When our attachments are healthy, the rest of our brain has a better chance to operate.

Assessment. Once something or someone has gotten the attention of level one, the information is passed along to the "guard shack" (the amygdala) at level two for a security screening. The amygdala stands guard over our attachments, offering three possible assessments about the "target": good, bad, or scary. These three opinions are entirely subjective, and permanent once formed. Anyone who has tried to battle the guard's opinions about heights, airplanes, or cocaine knows how unchanging these views can be. Evidence and persuasion get nowhere. Already operational at birth, this level begins developing opinions about chocolate, loud noises, elevators, airplanes, angry faces, dogs, or any other significant experience.

The assessment level produces the fight, flight, or freeze reactions. Something bad makes us want to fight. Something scary makes us want to flee or freeze. If we get triggered at this level, it can be hard for higher levels of the brain to function properly. This is why we do not do our most magnificent thinking when we are agitated or fearful.

When your amygdala gets triggered, it sends an alarm to the rest of the body, creating a high-energy state. This is why fear and anger feel like someone is stepping on your nervous system's gas pedal (whereas emotions like sadness or despair feel like someone is stepping on the brakes). If this alarm is louder than you have the capacity to handle, it can shut down the higher levels of brain activity or at least lower their capacity to function well.

Something good moves our joy elevator to the third floor of the brain. Likewise, having the maturity to suffer well keeps the elevator moving, fueled by the joy that "we've got this."

Attunement. The third floor of the brain reads relational signals from the world around us. This synchronization of operations has its headquarters in our cingulate cortex. By reading body language, energy levels, and movement, we can synchronize with other people and adapt to situations. Sharing a mental connection that is faster than words is crucial. Without this ability to attune to our world, we cannot form meaningful relationships, interact with others predictably, or understand what it means to be ourselves.

> The skill of synchronizing with others is one of the key elements of becoming a leader.

Tracking other people's minds in real time is a learned skill known as "mutual mind." We sense the mood of a friend or lock eyes with a colleague and carry on a conversation without words. We know what the other person is thinking. For example, you may have glanced at a coworker during a boring presentation and sent the message, "When will this end?" Both of you understood, even though nothing was said. You might even motion with your head to "Meet me in the hallway."

The skill of synchronizing with others is one of the key elements in becoming a leader. However, when leadership becomes overly focused on results and power (slow track), the ability to read others accurately (fast track) begins to deteriorate.

Training the attunement level of the brain gives us a better radar for reading people and situations. This is a crucial skill for leaders, who need to be able to sense the mood of their people and read the dynamics of their environment. Good attunement skills help us build stronger relationships, and strong relationships help us act like ourselves.

Action. The fourth floor of the joy elevator may just be the most important part of the brain. It is your brain's captain because—when it is properly developed—it has executive control over the rest of the brain. Level four of your brain thinks of itself as "me." We call it the action center because it is the captain that calls the shots and runs the brain. Having an elevator reach the captain is crucial for functioning well under stress. When well trained, the action center has the capacity to quiet our guard shack alarm (amygdala), direct our moral choices, be creative, think flexibly, and even influence such delicate functions as our immune system.

When the fourth-floor action center is strong enough, it has sufficient capacity to handle the upsets of life and return to joy regardless of what is happening at the levels below it. Enduring hardship well requires a well-developed action center that can resist becoming traumatized when things go badly. Instead, it maintains a strong, positive, and determined identity even when life is hard.

FOUR-LEVEL CONTROL CENTER

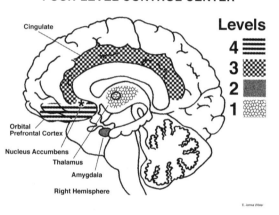

E. James Wilder

This top floor can also be thought of as the "joy bucket" of the brain. This is because it doubles as both the identity center and joy center of the brain. It is the identity center because it remembers who I am and how my people and I act when things get like this. Level four is the joy center because the brain grows increased density here with a proper workout routine of joy and peace. For as long as we live, this part of the brain can grow its capacity for joy.

BRAIN SCIENCE AND RARE HABITS

The four habits of rare leadership are anchored in the basics of the brain science we have learned so far.

1. **Remain relational.** The fast track (the first four levels of the joy elevator) is basically a relational machine. It is organized around attachment and craves joyful relationship. When it is operating properly, we find it relatively easy to remain relational.

2. **Act like yourself.** The top of the fast track (the prefrontal cortex) is the identity center of the brain. So when it is running well, we find it natural to remember who we are and how it is like us to act.

3. **Return to joy.** Since the top of the fast track is also the joy center, and since joy is the fuel the brain craves, it makes sense that when we are living as whole-brained, mature people, we return to joy quickly from upset emotions.

4. **Endure hardship well.** What really sets mature people apart from immature people is not simply that their brains can do these things, but that their brains are able to do these things even when life gets hard. They endure hardship well because they have the capacity to handle the weight of life and still remain relational, act like themselves, and return to joy.

THE POWER OF HABITS

Habits are formed as the brain performs certain functions over and over again. Eventually, neural pathways are formed, and a coating called "white matter" begins to develop around the pathways. White matter allows our brains to process information at superfast speeds up to two hundred times faster than normal brain function, which is already pretty fast! Habits (whether good or bad) form white matter in the brain that allows us to react to situations without taking the time to think about what we are doing. Breaking bad habits takes months because it requires building up new white matter around new habits strong enough to replace our old habits.

To understand the power of habits, it can be helpful to consider how important they are in activities like sports, music, and the arts. For example, hitting a major league fastball requires the brain to perform an incredible number of calculations in a split second. This requires the brain to develop enough white matter to make those neural connections rapidly and efficiently. It takes years of practice to build that amount of white matter in the brain. In the same way, our character—including our relational and emotional skills—is built around the habits we develop. If we develop good habits, white matter forms in our brain around those habits, and our good character and relational skills show up before we even think about them. If we develop bad habits, those habits often show up before we even realize what we are doing. This is why, when it comes to leadership, we often read that "the one with the best habits wins."

Most of us want solutions we can implement today. However, when it comes to maturity and learning new habits, the process can span months or even years—similar to learning a new language or mastering an instrument. It takes about one month for white matter to begin forming in our brains and even longer for white matter to get real traction. This book introduces you to important skills, but you will need to find people who can model those skills and invest time in intentional, repetitious practice to master the four RARE habits of emotional maturity. The maturity workouts at the end of each chapter are designed to help you jumpstart this process.

MATURITY WORKOUT: APPRECIATION

One of the fastest ways to grow your joy center is through the practice of appreciation. The goal of appreciation is to let yourself live in the feeling of gratitude for several minutes at a time. How often do we see a sunset and think, "That's pretty"? But there is a difference between noticing a pretty sunset and taking the time to sit down and enjoy it for a few minutes. Spending five minutes at a time in a state of appreciation can help to quiet your mind. It also helps grow your joy center.

Take five minutes twice a day for sixty days to practice appreciation. This will help you grow your capacity for joy, which also grows your capacity to handle hardship. To help you get started, use three simple categories for guiding your practice.

1. **Present**—What has happened in the last twenty-four hours that made you smile? Relive that moment or take time to enter into that moment. A good example of this is found in the movie *The Last Samurai* where the leader of the Samurai takes time to examine the cherry blossoms near his house. He is a leader carrying a tremendous amount of weight, yet he makes sure to take time every day to enjoy the little things in life—like the perfection of a cherry blossom.

2. **Future**—What do you have to look forward to in the next day or the next week? Are you going to see a friend? Go to a movie? Go out to dinner? Think of something you are anticipating that makes you smile, and let yourself dwell on that for a few minutes.

3. **Past**—Collect pictures and memorabilia of past moments of joy. It may relate to music, or sports, or vacations, or friends and family, or any other number of experiences that you remember as times of joy. Have a top-five list ready to go of happiest memories that you can revisit again and again.

Learning to live with joy is really not possible without appreciation. Growing this habit by building appreciation into your day, every day, will begin to grow your joy and thus your emotional capacity.

CHAPTER 3

Mature Leadership in Practice

TO GET A PICTURE of mature leadership in practice, consider this tale of two nursing units. Unit #1 was run by a veteran nurse who had become cynical from years of unmet expectations. She had little respect for the doctors, barely tolerated the patients, and could go on long rants about the families who came to see the patients. She was good at the technical part of her job, but dealing with emotions and relationships felt like a waste of time. When HR announced an appreciation initiative, it felt hypocritical—they didn't show her much appreciation—and pointless. People got paid! They just needed to do their jobs.[1]

Unit #2 was run by an innovator. This nurse had read some of Jim's material on the importance of joy and decided to take steps to build more joy into the culture. She introduced short training segments during staff times on simple ways to increase the joy levels on the unit. The nurses were taught to be relational before doing their work. It was a simple process.

- Look people in the eyes.
- Express curiosity.
- Go about your work.
- Smile!

It didn't take long to see results. Within two months patient approval ratings had skyrocketed 33 percent. The nurses noticed that doctors were quicker to make their rounds and seemed to like being on the floor. The relational atmosphere in this unit was contagious. Before long, other nurses were asking to be transferred there. By way of contrast, the first unit stayed pretty much the same.

A core priority that sets rare leaders apart from sandbox leaders is the commitment to building relational joy in the teams they lead. This doesn't mean they play games all day and make sure everyone is having fun. Joy is not about fun. It is about relational connection. When people feel connected with people who are happy to see them, they experience joy, and joy is the greatest motivator in the world. If you want a highly motivated team, you need a relationally bonded team, not one living in fear of the leader's mood swings.

Understanding the importance of relational joy in building a strong culture, I (Marcus) was struck by an interview I heard with Dabo Swinney, the head coach of the Clemson Tigers football team, after they won the 2018 national championship. Coach Swinney had taken a program that was an afterthought in the ACC and turned them into a perennial powerhouse. In the interview after the championship game, Swinney said that his word for the year had been joy. That got my attention. He wanted his team to play with joy. Zach Lenz in *Sports Illustrated* explained it this way: "Whether it is wins and losses or pressure from a rabid fanbase, there are a number of things that can try to steal your joy." Dabo credited his personal joy to his relationship with Jesus, then he went on to say, "When you get a young group of people that believe, are passionate, that love each other, that sacrifice, and that are committed to a purpose, you'd better look out—great things can happen, and that's what you saw tonight."[2]

Here was a leader who understood the high-octane power of joy and was intentional about prioritizing joy in the culture he built. Notice that passion, love, and sacrifice are all natural outgrowths of a joy-fueled culture. People will do hard things and make great sacrifices when they have joy in their relationships.

LEADERS: CREATING ENGAGEMENT IN WHAT MATTERS

Building on the brain science in the last chapter, we believe a definition of leadership needs to reflect both the work of the fast track and the slow track. The slow track excels at focus and problem solving. It is good at getting tasks done related to what matters most in the moment. The fast track specializes in relational connection. It tracks the world around it, identifies what is important whether it is good, bad, or scary, and lets the slow track know where to put its focus. Part of what sets great leaders apart is their ability to "read" the lay of the land and recognize where the spotlight needs to be focused. This ability to read people, situations, groups, and moods is all fast-track stuff. It exists because of the Skills and Habits (SH) we have developed throughout our lives.

Combining these activities leads us to define leadership as "creating engagement in what matters." Great leaders need to be good at both recognizing what matters and creating engagement around that focus. Some leaders are good at creating engagement, but they aren't very good at identifying what really matters, especially when they are upset. Other leaders can quickly assess what really matters but lack the ability to create engagement to get anything done about it. Well-developed Skills and Habits (SH) in the fast track will increase both a leader's ability to define what matters and to create engagement. The more RARE habits you develop, the greater the capacity you will have for effective leadership.

HOW THE BRAIN DEFINES WHAT MATTERS

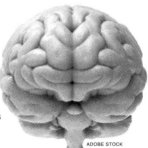

RIGHT
FAST TRACK
RADAR

Notices what
is important
and determines
the path of least
damage, then signals
the slow track
to focus.

LEFT
SLOW TRACK
SPOTLIGHT

Drills down
on what the
fast track sensed
was the path of
least damage.

ADOBE STOCK

DEFINING WHAT MATTERS

Defining what matters involves both the right and left hemispheres of the brain. The radar on the right side of the brain notices what is important, determines the path of least damage, and signals the slow track to shine its spotlight on the tasks related to that issue.

Many of the tasks most commonly associated with leadership are slow track activities. The slow track gives Conscious Attention (CA) to such things as:

- Vision
- Mission
- Strategy
- Analytics
- Planning
- Accountability

If you think back to CASHCoW in chapter 1, defining what matters is directed through Conscious Attention (CA). This part of leadership shines a spotlight on what is most important at this moment. It is about focus. Focus needs to be firmly anchored in a well-developed fast track to identify what matters and direct effective action. Conscious Attention (the slow track) can drill down on details, solve problems, direct energy, implement change, improve and extend helpful activities, and coordinate timing. This fifth and final stage of mental processing excels at focusing, but it needs help to know where to focus.

Knowing where to focus is the job of the Skills and Habits (SH) we have accumulated in our fast track. Leaders with well-developed Skills and Habits are able to "size up" situations quickly and intuitively determine where their Conscious Attention (CA) needs to focus. The fast track is like a radar that sees the big picture and picks out what is important. It then sends a message to the slow track, so it can shine its spotlight on what is important and deal with it. The more developed the Skills and Habits (SH) in a leader's fast track processor become, the more effective the leader will be in knowing where to focus.

TOXIC MOTIVATION

Unfortunately, immature leaders often fail to create engagement with joy. Instead, they resort to toxic motivation. There are six primary emotions that drive this type of motivation.

- Fear
- Anger
- Shame
- Disgust
- Sadness
- Hopeless despair

As a leader, if I do not know how to remain relational, act like myself, and return to joy from any of these emotions, I will find myself avoiding them or using them to manipulate others. For example, one leader tried to shame me (Jim) into volunteering for an important project. But I knew how to act like myself and return to joy when faced with shame, so the motivational tactic didn't work. The man finally blurted out, "You just refuse to feel shame, don't you?" It wasn't that I didn't know how to feel shame. I just wasn't controlled by it. It was obvious that this leader had learned to rely on others to fear the feeling of shame in order to motivate them to do what he wanted.

Predatory leaders often learn which emotions trigger fear in their coworkers. Then they use those emotions to motivate engagement. If fear works, they rely on that. If anger or disgust gets a reaction, they will use those. Toxic motivation works when people do not know how to return to joy from those emotions. As a leader, if I am unable to return to joy from any of these emotions, I will be more easily manipulated by others because I fear feeling that way myself or dealing with others who express that emotion. All toxic motivations come from fearing how we are going to feel. This fear then keeps us from acting like our true selves.

Here is a quick assessment you can use to evaluate your maturity level related to the big six negative emotions.

Fear

- What fears motivate me or my associates to work harder?
- What fears interfere with work because they cause me or my associates to avoid people, situations, or tasks?

Examples: Failure, loss of job, loss of status, upsetting someone, having someone upset with me, fatigue, damage to mission, damage to my/our image, how I will feel if . . .

Avoidance

- Which of these emotions do I most avoid?
- Which do I see my colleagues avoiding?
- Which am I most likely to warn colleagues about?

Results

- Which of these emotions do I most often use to motivate myself when I need results?
- Which of these emotions do I most often use to motivate others when I need results?

There are skill clusters we can learn that help with both motivation and performance. One of the most important clusters is related to motivating people without overwhelming them because performance drops when people get fatigued or burned out. We need to (1) quiet ourselves when we feel overwhelmed (see maturity workout #1); and (2) we need to recognize when the group or someone in the group is starting to feel overwhelmed, so we can take a breather to restore our energy.

When we practice these simple skills, it allows us to keep performance high, synchronized, on task, and productive.

A second skill cluster is related to team building. The

main purpose of these skills is to produce focused and sustainable unity of mind, effort, and energy as the team learns to synchronize. This skill cluster combines knowing when to stop so that we don't overwhelm people and building relational connection as a team. There are three practical ways to build positive connections.

Share joy—Just as the high-joy nursing unit learned to share joy that created engagement through smiles, curiosity, and kindness, so teams that regularly share joy with one another grow more bonded.

Express appreciation—Demonstrating authentic appreciation on a regular basis helps build trust in the team.

Form protective bonds—Families protect each other. One of the ways we build a strong team is by developing the skill of seeing each other as people to be protected and cared for.

The art of creating joyful engagement requires both avoiding toxic motivation and increasing the development of the skills that help our teams avoid overwhelm and grow trusting attachments.

WHAT RARE LEADERS DO WITHOUT THINKING

We've been looking at Conscious Attention (CA)—what leaders think and talk about. But what makes leaders great comes from all the things they do without thinking about them.

This is their map to working with people. What leaders do without thinking about it is made of Skills and Habits (SH) that run so quickly and automatically the leader does not even notice them most of the time. As a result, leaders rarely mention and often cannot explain their Skills and Habits. Our purpose in this book is to reveal this rare skill set, and show what it contains and how it is built.

One of my (Marcus) coworkers went to a leadership conference that featured two best-selling authors. When he got back, I asked for his biggest takeaway from the event. He said, "If I was wired like those two guys, I'd be a success too." What he was getting at was the principle we are describing here. The success of these two leaders wasn't really the result of the principles they were explaining, it was the result of the Skills and Habits they had developed over a lifetime that they used every day without conscious thought. Like many leaders, they did not articulate what really set them apart because it flowed through their brains faster than conscious thought. Others, using only the conscious process discussed in the conference, would not have the same success.

> "If I was wired like those two guys, I'd be a success too."

I (Jim) made the same observation about therapist workshops. Presenters often explained the processes they found effective, but when others tried to implement those processes they did not find them effective. This was because they did not have the same fast-track skills and habits as the presenters. The presenters themselves often did not realize that it was these habits of character and relational skill more than their processes that made them work.

HOW TO CREATE JOYFUL ENGAGEMENT

There are at least four practical ways leaders can create joyful engagement in the people they lead. We know we have succeeded in this task when we hear people say things like, "I sure like this team and what we do." To build this kind of engagement we need to practice the four Ps:

1. **Prioritize Group Identity.** Rare leaders want results, but that is not their focus. They plan for results, but their focus is on the identity of their group. The primary job of the leader is to help the team know who they are and how it is like them to act. This means the leader needs to model that identity, communicate that identity, and embed that identity into the values and practices of the team.

   For example, if you run a restaurant, is your primary focus making money, or is your primary focus creating a great dining experience? If you focus on the money, you might cut corners that cheapen the experience. In the end, you could end up losing money by forgetting your identity. The leader's #1 task is making sure the group remembers who they are and how it is like you to act.

   A group identity is a powerful force. It is a far more transformational force than accountability. Once I know who my people are, I am much more inclined to act like them, to think like them, to sacrifice for them, and come to their defense when I feel my people are under attack. We see this in politics, religion, race relations, gender issues, and in many other aspects of life. An identity group can promote good values or bad ones, but either way it is a powerful transformative force. Any leader who wants to see real change needs to make forming a strong group identity the top priority.

2. **Promote Belonging.** Perhaps the first step in building a strong group identity is creating a clear path to belonging. That process may start with a clear statement that you are hired, or you made the team, but there is far more to it than that. People need to know that they are part of a relational system that is set up to help them succeed. They need relational training and mentoring. They need to know there are others invested in seeing them grow. If you just give people a task list and hold them accountable for achieving results, but you don't give them the resources, encouragement, and training they need to succeed, they are going to feel disconnected and unvalued.

> People need to know that they are part of a relational system that is set up to help them succeed.

An important element of belonging is knowing that you are not alone with your problems. If you have been in the military (or even seen movies about the military), you know that when units form a strong sense of identity and belonging, they take care of each other. They will literally risk their lives to make sure their people don't have to go through their problems alone. The twin elements of identity and belonging work together to create a culture of transformation that blows away what can be accomplished through accountability alone.

3. **Practice Authentic Appreciation.*** Mature leaders are good at noticing effort, process, and improvement. They don't just notice results. They notice attitude and find actions worthy of praise. One of the ways a leader creates an identity for the group is by what gets praised. If you notice and appreciate effort and attitude, people learn, "We are the sort of people who give maximum effort and display great attitude." If you simply tell people to give great effort and have a great attitude, but you only show appreciation for results, your team will get the message that you don't really care about anything but winning. While that may sound good, it isn't. Leaders who focus only on results suck the joy out of the process and create no end of problems that will need to be overcome later. On the other hand, leaders who show authentic appreciation for the steps along the

---

* Dr. Paul White, coauthor of *5 Languages of Appreciation in the Workplace* and other bestselling books on building healthy relationships with and among employees, has done much to popularize this concept.

way, and not just the destination, inspire and motivate to greater effort.

4. **Protect the Weak.** One of the most crucial differences between maturity and immaturity is one's attitude toward weakness. Immature people hide their own weaknesses because they don't know how to deal with shame. They also see the weaknesses of others as an opportunity for self-benefit. When a person becomes predatory, they view weakness as an opportunity to attack. They no longer care about the other person. They only care about winning.

I (Marcus) worked alongside many people who excelled at tracking the weaknesses of others. They didn't constantly use people's weakness against them, only when they felt threatened. In one case, I had a coworker who gained a reputation for throwing people under the bus whenever he felt blamed for something that went wrong. This leader had a habit of saying things like, "You are right. As the leader this is my fault, *but . . .*" There was always a "but." Nothing was ever his fault, and to prove it, he could list off all the weaknesses and failures of his team members to show why the blame (and shame) belonged to someone else.

> There was always a "but." Nothing was ever his fault.

In prior writings, I (Jim) coined a set of terms for three common approaches to weakness: **possums, predators, and protectors.** Possums are people who know they are weak.

Their one "superpower" is playing dead. Their motto is, "I don't do confrontation." A good day for a possum is one where no feathers get ruffled and no one gets their feelings hurt.

Predators are the reason possums exist. These are strong people who use their strength to stay at the top of the pecking order. They track the weaknesses of others, so they know where to attack if they ever feel threatened. Sometimes predators attack weak people in their sphere of influence just to reinforce who is on top.

Protectors are mature leaders who protect possums from predators and make it safe to contribute and grow. You cannot create joyful engagement if a culture becomes predatory. The protectors have to dominate the culture.

To illustrate this, think of two locker rooms. One is run by protectors, the other by predators. What happens to the possums (those who are weak) in a locker room run by predators? They get bullied, don't they? The predators may justify their bullying and claim they just wanted to toughen someone up, when in reality they just wanted to reinforce their position at the top of the food chain. This happens beyond the locker room in all sorts of settings from boardrooms to classrooms to cubicles. In contrast to this, what happens to the weak in a locker room run by protectors? They get help. Protectors find ways to help the weak grow stronger.

As the leader of an organization, I (Marcus) have tried to create a culture in which people express their weakness and ask for help. Part of every staff meeting is asking people what problems they are facing that the rest of the team can help solve. In one case, a staff member was spending too much time doing spreadsheets because they weren't good at it. We were able to help them by finding someone else to do the spreadsheet work, which freed them up to do the content creation and strategic planning that were more critical to our mission. One of our leaders recognized that another staff member was struggling at a new job. He took it upon himself to set up a series of meetings to determine what was wrong and the kind of help that was needed. By offloading some tasks to other people and helping develop a clear process for this particular assistant, everyone's productivity increased.

Protecting the weak doesn't mean enabling weakness. It means creating an environment that encourages growth. However, there are times when even rare leaders need to fire people for non-performance or lack of fit with the group. I (Marcus) once had to fire someone not so much for poor performance but for the lack of ownership for that performance. In this case, the problem was that the person would not ask for help but blamed others for their poor performance and routinely hid information that might make them look bad. Such behavior undermined trust and was having a negative impact on the workplace environment. I had to let one person go to keep from losing the culture we were trying to build.

HOW DO YOU DO THIS? BUILDING SKILLS AND HABITS

Brain science teaches us that leadership is creating engagement in what matters. Mature leaders are masters at creating engagement around relational joy. They have built fast-track skills and habits that allow them to run their own lives on the fuel of joy and they bring that same type of engagement to everything they do.

> Leadership is creating engagement in what matters.

Effective leadership requires three systems to be operating simultaneously. We learned these systems in the first chapter as focus, habits, and collaboration (remembered as CASHCoW):

Conscious Attention (CA)—This is your ability to do focused work. The left side of your brain (the slow track) excels at focusing on tasks that need to be done and problems that need to be solved. The fast track shines a spotlight on what needs your conscious attention and your slow track takes over and starts getting work done.

Skills and Habits (SH)—The right side of your brain (the fast track) is like a radar system that detects where the spotlight needs to shine. Mature leaders have well-developed skills and habits in the fast track that help them intuitively recognize where attention is needed. This is why some aspects of leadership can't be taught as principles. At the fast track level, there are skills and habits that have to be learned so that they show up without having to think about them.

Collaborative Work (CoW)—Creating engagement requires us to be able to engage in collaborative work. We work with peers, supervisors, clients, and many others. Mature leaders who bring well-developed RARE habits to these relationships will find it much easier to engage in collaborative work.

If we are struggling to create a "CASHCoW Culture," the most common reason is not a lack of focus, but a lack of skills and habits. We encourage you to do the maturity workouts as you go through this book as a good way to start building those skills. It is also essential to work on them with a group if they are going to become habits that show up without thinking about them.

MATURITY WORKOUT: APPRECIATING OTHERS

A simple exercise for growing your relational maturity is to practice authentic appreciation. Start looking for attitudes and actions that you appreciate and share that appreciation. Even if you don't like everything about someone or feel disgust for their level of competence, you can look for something that you truly appreciate. But avoid sarcasm. Don't say something like, "I truly appreciate your genius for getting other people to do your work." That is not authentic appreciation!

Here are some practical ways you can let people know you appreciate them—different approaches work better with different people, so it is helpful to pay attention to what means the most to each person.

1. **Public recognition.** Just like a coach awards a game ball at the end of a football game, so it can be helpful to publicly acknowledge people who model the attitudes or the actions that embody the group's values.

2. **Personal notes.** My father was a college president who taught me (Marcus) to never put criticism in writing. He said, "If you have something critical to say, share it face to face. But if you have something to praise or something to appreciate, put it in writing."

3. **Symbolic rewards.** People are motivated by more than just money. A token that suggests they were noticed doing something right can mean a lot. The token doesn't have to cost a lot, but it needs to symbolize honor, so that people feel like they are being honored when they get it. Be creative. You can even create excuses to give out awards.

4. **Eye contact, a handshake, and a clear "thank you."** This means more to some people than anything else.

CHAPTER 4

Remain Relational

EVERYONE DEALS WITH PROBLEMS. One of the key characteristics that separates mature leaders from sandbox leaders is their ability to remain relational when they deal with problems. One project manager who learned this lesson wrote the following words on the whiteboard in his office. "Keep relationships bigger than problems." The phrase was written in big letters above his desk. Needless to say, this started a lot of conversations. People would ask, "What does that mean?" It would give him a chance to explain that in their line of work there would always be problems to solve— but there was a way of solving problems that was relational and a way of solving problems that damaged relationships. He wanted it to be clear up front that no matter how big the problem, his goal was to handle that problem in a way that valued the relationship and not just the solution.

In this chapter we want to introduce some key concepts and practices that help us keep relationships bigger than problems.

THE DIMMER SWITCH AND ENEMY MODE

The fast track in our brain has something in it that can be thought of as a dimmer switch. As joy levels drop, so does the power that runs the joy elevator. When everything is working well and the switch is on, it is easy to feel and act like ourselves. As joy drops, even mildly upsetting emotions can begin dimming the activity of our relational circuits. I feel less like "myself" and lose the capacity to remain relational. When our emotions become overwhelming, the switch goes off. The joy elevator stops. This is bad.

When the joy switch goes off, we lose access to the part of our brain that remembers who we are and how it is like us to act. Our fast track reacts like a muscle with a cramp. Without access to our identity center, we act like a different person when we are upset. As a result, our slow track has to take over handling our relationships and emotions.

The slow track is good at problem solving, but it is not designed to deal with relationships. It sees people as problems to be solved and focuses on managing others to maximize winning. Because the slow track has no ability to be relational, it will manage relationships rather than form attachments. In some cases, our slow track doesn't just see people as problems to solve (which is bad enough), it sees them as enemies to defeat. When this happens, our brains go into **"enemy mode."** Enemy mode sees people as problems that should do what we say, leave us alone, and not cause trouble. In enemy mode we see people as prey to use or destroy. As a result, we want them to do what we say, leave us alone, and not cause trouble.

There are two kinds of enemy mode: intelligent and stupid. Stupid enemy mode happens when we hurt people because we aren't thinking about the consequences of our behavior. When our relational circuits go completely offline, we hurt people without thinking about what we are doing. We just act stupid and usually regret it later. Intelligent enemy mode is predatory. It tracks weaknesses in others so it knows where and when to attack for maximum advantage. People who function in intelligent enemy mode value winning over relationships. They intentionally set about to seduce, manipulate, dominate, and harm others. In this mode, a person can be charming and very relational, but it is calculated. Predators use their relational skills to get what they want, with no concern for the damage it does to others.

RELATIONAL CIRCUITS IN THE BRAIN

The fast track is home to the relational circuits (RCs) in your brain. When these circuits are on, we naturally remain relational and act like ourselves. When these circuits shut down we lose access to the action center (aka the captain) at the top of the fast track. As you may recall, the action center is the part of the brain that thinks of itself as "me." If we lose access to this part of the brain, we will handle emotions and relationships in a way that is not like us and not very relational.

A branch manager of a large investment company had

modeled how to remain relational when facing a big problem. He had an employee who made a serious mistake. With a mixture of fear and courage, this employee came into the manager's office to let him know she had accidentally sold shares of stock for a client when she had been asked to buy. The mistake had cost everyone thousands of dollars. She came into the room expecting this leader to react like her old boss—a man who frequently slipped into enemy mode. She expected a temper tantrum, a good shaming, and possibly termination from her job. Instead, the leader remained relational as he dealt with the problem. He took time to remember what he appreciated about this woman's approach to work and why he had hired her in the first place. By pausing and keeping his relational circuits on, he was able to keep his head and have a productive conversation about what needed to happen next. He then reassured her that he was happy to have her on the team and expected great things in the future. She started to cry. She was overwhelmed at his reaction. The maturity he demonstrated in this situation demonstrated the kind of mature leadership that creates trust, joy, and engagement in the people we lead.

> For her mistake, she expected a tantrum, a good shaming, and possibly termination.

CONTROLLING THE DIMMER SWITCH

The following checklist can help us identify when our dimmer switch has started shutting down our brain's relational circuits (RCs). If we can check off any of these boxes, it means our RCs are not on and we are going to be trapped dealing with life with only half of our brain (the slow track).

- I want to make a person or feeling go away.
- I want to fight, flee, or freeze.
- I feel like it is your fault when I hurt your feelings.
- When others are talking, I am already figuring out what to say before they finish.
- I don't want to make eye contact.
- People are a bother and/or get in my way.

Once we recognize that our switch is off, our slow track has a new problem to solve: How do we get our relational circuits back on? To help us do this, we recommend a simple process called CAKE—Curiosity, Appreciation, Kindness, and Eye contact. The process of getting our dimmer switch back on is pretty straightforward.

1. **Focus on the problem of getting our RCs back on.** To do this, we need to look away from the person momentarily and remind ourselves that the first problem we need to solve is how to stay relational.

2. **Find a solution** (find a piece of CAKE). We need to ask ourselves:
   - Is there anything in this conversation about which I have genuine curiosity?
   - Is there anything about this person I appreciate?

- Is there any way I can show some kindness?

3. **Focus on the person again.** Once we recover one of these three qualities, we should make eye contact and re-engage with the conversation.

Sometimes resetting our dimmer switch is (pardon the pun) a piece of cake because it happens without even thinking about it. Other times we need some space and time to recover before we can get our relational circuits back on. Let us examine the elements more carefully.

Curiosity. Curiosity is a genuine interest in what someone thinks or feels. One of the most common reasons we lose curiosity is that we think we already have someone figured out. We are convinced we already know what they think and how they feel, so we justify disengaging. When this happens, it is easy to tune out the other person and start thinking about something else.

Appreciation. Appreciation doesn't mean we like everything about someone. It means there is something about them we genuinely admire or something about your relationship that is good. When our circuits dim, we can forget what we like about someone pretty quickly. This happens in all of our relationships—at work and at home. When someone is actively pushing our buttons and getting on our nerves, it can be very hard to remember anything we appreciate about them.

Kindness. Kindness is the act of doing something good for another person. When our RCs are on, it is usually easy to think of ways to do something helpful for another person or something they would like. When our RCs shut down, being kind can be the last thing on our mind.

Eye contact. Avoiding eye contact is a common sign that our RCs are off. Maintaining eye contact is a good way to keep our relational circuits engaged. When we realize there are no pieces of CAKE left—we can't find any curiosity, appreciation, or kindness, and we don't want to make eye contact—our relational circuits are definitely off and we have a problem to solve. At that point, it is best to take a break before trying to re-engage relationally.

A friend of mine (Marcus)—we'll call him Bill—told me about a story of how CAKE helped him in a very concrete way with a sales call he had to make. He called a client who had placed a large order every year for several years, only to find out they were not going to be buying anything that year. Bill's immediate reaction was a mixture of fear and anger. However, he had just read about CAKE and remaining relational that very day. He decided to engage with curiosity. He asked the client, "So . . . what is going on over there? Is everything okay? This seems like a pretty big change."

The man admitted that everyone was feeling a lot of stress and that there were in-house issues driving the decision. Bill took the time to validate the emotion and show empathy for the situation. He then expressed his appreciation for the man's vulnerability and for their business through the years. By remaining relational, Bill helped his client quiet his upset emotions and start feeling like himself. After a few minutes, the client changed his mind and placed an order after all. Bill contacted me right away to say thanks for introducing him to CAKE and the idea of remaining relational under stress. He was sure he would have lost the sale without that guidance. Of course, remaining relational doesn't guarantee positive results. But over time, people who handle themselves like adults and endure hardship well usually do well because people like doing business with them.

ENVELOPE CONVERSATIONS: DON'T LEAD WITH PROBLEMS

An important aspect of remaining relational while enduring hardship has to do with conflict management. When we need to address problems, it is important to keep the relationship bigger than the problem. This means we want to keep our relational circuits on while we are problem solving. An envelope conversation is a simple model for remaining relational while addressing problems. You can think of it as slipping the problem into the envelope of relationship.

Too often we lead with problems when we talk to people. There is a time for doing this. It is called a crisis. But if we constantly lead with problems and don't take the time to remain relational, we quickly turn everything into a crisis, which wears people out. Instead of leading with the problem, an envelope conversation leads with relational history and ends with the goal of keeping the working relationship on good terms. The problem gets sandwiched between these two slices of relational bread.

- **State your relational history.** How well do you know this person? How much history do you have together? Start with a statement about your relational history. However, you don't want to say something like "We've worked together for eight years and you've always been a jerk." That's not what we mean by relational history. You want to say something neutral or positive, like "We've worked together for several years now." Or, "I know we just met, and I'd like us to get off on a good note."

- **State the problem.** "Your report made it sound like I was to blame for the team missing the deadline." Or, "I didn't appreciate the way you talked to me in the meeting we just had."

- **State your hope for a positive relational future.** The goal here is to look for a solution to the problem that allows you to work together in the future with a greater degree of trust. You might say, "I'd like us to have a good working relationship, so we can collaborate effectively moving forward." Or, "I hope we can resolve this in a way that is helpful to both of us."

Learning how to have envelope conversations can make it easier to confront problems instead of letting them fester. Several people have told us that they are much quicker to confront people now that they know how to do it relationally. The result is that more problems are being addressed and greater trust is being built in these relationships.

One business owner who learned about envelope conversations had a chance to practice the skill with a veteran operations manager. We'll call him Joe. The owner was preparing to retire and leave his son in charge of the business. He decided to take a few weeks off and let his son practice running the company. The problem was that the veteran operations guy did not respect his son and made that clear to the rest of the staff. He ignored the son's leadership while the owner was gone. It was a situation that needed to be addressed when the owner got back from vacation. In the past, the owner had been known for his quick temper and leading with problems in such conversations. This time he decided to keep the relationship bigger than the problem and used an envelope conversation. It went something like this.

History: "Joe, we've worked together for nearly thirty years. We've been through a lot together and you've contributed a great deal to the growth of this company."

Problem: "Here is the issue. I'm not leaving the company to you. I'm leaving it to my son. We have got to find a way for you two to work together better."

Future: "I'm confident we can work this out in a way that

will benefit everyone and keep this relationship strong for years to come."

The results were encouraging. Joe admitted he could handle things better and agreed to mentor the son rather than ignore him. Since learning how to have envelope conversations, this man told me he is less afraid to deal with confrontation because he is learning how to keep the relationship bigger than the problem.

BEING THE KIND OF LEADER PEOPLE WANT TO FOLLOW

Remaining relational while solving problems builds trust in the people we lead. It is one of the core skills and habits from the CASHCoW model that needs to start showing up automatically if we want to become the kind of leader people love to follow. Understanding the importance of relational circuits and the brain's dimmer switch can give you a paradigm for understanding what it means to remain relational. Practicing skills like CAKE and using processes like envelope conversations can help us grow this habit and increase our relational maturity.

MATURITY WORKOUT:
RELATIONAL CIRCUIT TRAINING

Learning to recognize when our relational circuits have gone off and taking steps to get them back on is crucial to growing our relational maturity. The exercise for dealing with this is to track when our RCs go off and use CAKE to get them back on.

1. Track and record times this week when your RCs go off. Write them out on a computer document or in a journal of some kind. Look for patterns. Are there particular emotions that trigger your RCs to shut down more than others?

2. When you notice your RCs going off, practice using at least one of the CAKE skills to get them back on. In a couple of sentences, record the differences you observe between conversations you have with your RCs on and your RCs off.

3. You might also work intentionally on a specific CAKE skill. For example, you might choose to focus on practicing curiosity. Curiosity expresses genuine interest in the emotions and perspectives of other people. Authenticity is key.

4. Was there a conversation recently in which your relational circuits went off? How would that conversation have gone differently if you had practiced curiosity?

5. Is it possible to follow up on that conversation and use curiosity more intentionally?

CHAPTER 5

Act Like Yourself

TO "ACT LIKE YOURSELF" means acting like an adult. Adults are strong people who are tender toward weakness. They have the strength to stand up for themselves and not get pushed around. Adults are not doormats. They are not easy to manipulate or intimidate. However, there is more to adult maturity than strength. Adults use their strength to serve. They don't just look out for themselves; they look out for their people.

Earlier in the book, we introduced the idea of possums, predators, and protectors. Possums are people who do not live with adult maturity because they are not strong enough. They have not developed the skills and habits to endure hardship well. Predators have the strength that possums lack, but they are not living with adult maturity. They use their strength only for their own interests. Protectors are strong people who notice the needs of others and are willing to stand up to predators when necessary.

Protector leadership reminds me (Marcus) of the many

Westerns I have seen on TV or in the theater. A typical storyline begins with a band of cutthroats who control a town with fear and intimidation. These predator leaders dominate the culture until the hero (a protector leader) shows up and comes to the aid of those who lack the strength to do so themselves. Both the predator and the protector are strong, but one uses their strength selfishly, the other uses their strength to serve. In Westerns like these, and in real life, a hero often doesn't see himself (or herself) as heroic. The hero often says something like, "I just did what anyone would do in this situation." The reason heroes often don't see their behavior as extraordinary is that they are just acting like themselves. The hardship hasn't changed who they are or how it is like them to act.

But how do we build a strong identity?

KNOWING WHAT SATISFIES

A strong identity requires knowing what satisfies. In order to act like yourself, you need to know who you are. Many of us were not raised with a healthy sense of identity. Some repair work may be needed. One of the keys to a strong identity is learning to distinguish what is satisfying from what is merely temporarily pleasurable. Something is satisfying when it still makes you smile several days later. When something is merely temporarily pleasurable, it is fun at the moment, but you do not revisit that moment with any great sense of satisfaction or fulfillment. If I spend half of my afternoon playing Solitaire on the computer, that may be fun, but I am not likely to revisit that afternoon in my mind with a sense of joy. On the other hand, if I spend half of the afternoon doing something creative and relational, I can revisit that memory again and again and relive the sense of satisfaction.

Learning what satisfies provides an important clue to what it means to be you. For example, I (Marcus) like sports, history, and home improvement projects. I have many fond memories of my days as an athlete and still look forward to playing golf or tennis. I wrote a book on the history of Rome just for fun, and I feel a lot of satisfaction when I recall building a deck with my daughter, painting a bedroom with my son's help, and discussing house designs with my wife. Expanding the list of activities we enjoy helps us grow our world and what it means to be ourselves in this world. I (Jim) have mastered many skills that bring me a great deal of satisfaction, like mountain climbing, deep sea diving, playing the guitar, birdwatching, photography, and more. Mastering such skills is far more satisfying than, say, binge-watching Netflix and eating ice cream.

Spending time doing satisfying work and engaging in satisfying relationships not only helps build our sense of identity, it helps us bring balance and rhythm to life. Leaders who constantly push themselves and make their life all about work burn themselves out and/or burn out other people. However, leaders who fill their lives with satisfying activity and relational balance run on the fuel of joy.

As we have seen, Denmark is consistently listed as one of the happiest countries in the world. Danes value relationships, proper rest, sharing meals, spending time out of doors. Leaders—and the rest of us—could learn from their example.

BELONGING

A strong identity requires belonging. From our brain's perspective, our identity is anchored in belonging. Our identity comes from who our people are. Consider the following examples.

- **Executives.** If "our people" are executives, it means we see ourselves as belonging to this group. The idea of being an executive comes with a set of presuppositions and expectations about what it means to belong to such a group. We form our expectations of what it means to belong to such a group based on examples we have seen. When you think of the "executives," what comes to mind? Is it a good thing or a bad thing to be an executive? How do I expect executives to act around employees? How do I expect executives to handle confrontation? How is it like executives to deal with risk? Embracing the identity "executive" means that our values flow from a sense of belonging to this group.

- **Engineers.** If "our people" are engineers, we have a pretty good idea of who our people are and how it is like us to act. Within our group, we also know who we want to imitate and whose characteristics we want to avoid. Growing our competence within this identity group requires watching how others go about their business and imitating those who do things well. Forming relationships with people who bring out the best in us is the surest way to grow.

It should be clear where this is going. Whether we are talking about teachers, writers, nurses, police officers, counselors, politicians, or mechanics, there is a clear identity that comes from belonging to a group. Within these larger categories are

> Forming relationships with people who bring out the best in us is the surest way to grow.

subcategories that help define who we are and who our people are. Effective leaders surround themselves with people who model skills they want to learn. Effective leaders are also intentional about the kind of culture they want to build in the group they lead and they understand that culture is best taught by example and not simply through accountability.

The first time I (Marcus) remember being aware of the power of belonging and identity was when I played high school basketball on one of the best teams in the state of Indiana. First, there was a clear identity that came from being part of the team. People saw me differently because of my group. I saw myself differently. I was part of a heritage of excellence. Our school had won two state championships, produced several All-State performers, and had won seven of the past eight sectional titles. Success was an expectation, and part of our identity. Secondly, within the team there was a culture of excellence. As a sophomore, I saw how hard the seniors worked in practice. I saw the respect they showed the coaches. I watched how they handled themselves around other students. I saw things I liked and things I wanted to do differently, but I clearly saw the expectation of excellence played out all around me. Belonging to the team instilled an identity that helped me understand, "This is how my people go about their business."

> Culture is best taught by example and not simply through accountability.

I had a similar experience in my first internship. My first day on the job, the lead manager gave me a leather-bound calendar and assigned me to a mentor. He told me to attend staff meeting, then have lunch with my mentor to get coached in time management. It was pretty easy to see what was valued by "my people."

TESTING

A strong identity requires testing. Groups that go through hardship together and come out on the other side will always be stronger than groups who avoid the struggle. Facing difficult situations as a team not only knits people together but molds the character of the group both collectively and individually.

In some ways we don't know who we are until we go through the fire. Identity is forged in battle after battle as we learn to endure hardship with our people. The more often we face what we fear and recover, the stronger we get and the harder it is for hardship to cause us to turn into someone we are not.

Whether we face lawsuits, attacks on social media, betrayal in the office, failure, or any number of other hardships, the more often we make it through the pain, the more developed our identity becomes.

THE STRONG SENSE OF SELF

When I (Marcus) first heard Jim say that maturity meant acting like yourself, I thought he was nuts. Most of the people I knew who said, "I'm just acting like myself" were doing something really stupid. What Jim helped me understand is that "acting like yourself" really means you are living with the identity center of your brain in control of your emotions. The people who justified foolish behavior by claiming they were just being themselves were actually malfunctioning. They were simply demonstrating the lack of development in their fast track.

The leaders we trust and respect are the ones who have such a well-developed sense of identity, they don't have to constantly prove themselves or be the center of attention. Their strong sense of self means they are free to serve others and take care of their people. Because they have a well-practiced sense of identity, they have the character to endure hardship and be okay. This kind of maturity can't be developed overnight. It requires going through numerous battles with your people and coming out stronger and more bonded as a result.

MATURITY WORKOUT:
FORMING A PERSONAL IDENTITY GROUP

As we noted earlier in the book, the most powerful transformational tool in the world is an identity group. As a leader you not only want to form your team into an identity group, you need to belong to your own identity group—one that can help you keep growing as a person.

We often hear that it is lonely at the top. There is always some truth to this in terms of the weight of decision-making, but too often as leaders we become completely isolated relationally. We don't have a group we think of as "my people." This is not good. You need people in your life who are on a growth journey like yours.

1. Identify people who challenge you to be better. Ask yourself, "Who do I need in my life if I am going to become the best version of myself this year?" Create a list of people you can connect with virtually or in person who might welcome the opportunity to be

part of a group built on vulnerability and empathy. It may not be safe to do this with coworkers at first, but it is important to have a group that begins to form a sense of belonging and an identity as people who are working on developing RARE habits.

2. Create an identity statement. Here is an example. "We are rare leaders. We encourage each other to remain relational, act like ourselves, and return to joy when we endure hardship. We are protectors. We see weakness in others and look for ways to help. We see weakness in ourselves and ask for help. We see those who abuse weakness and intervene."

3. Follow the four S's of healthy groups.

- **Stories**—Learn one another's stories. Over the course of months and years, you should know one another's stories at more profound levels. You don't need to fix each other. But the more that people are seen and heard and met with empathy, the closer the bonds become.

- **Service**—Find ways to work together to make life good for someone else. Your identity group should be a force for good that bonds together through serving others.

- **Study**—Choose books to study together that keep you on the path to maturity development. A couple of books that take a similar approach to this one are *The Pandora Problem* and *The Joy Switch*.

- **Socialize**—Visit each other's homes if possible. Meet for dinner. Go camping. Go golfing. Create ways to spend time together as friends doing things people enjoy. It is especially beneficial to bond around learning new skills together. For example, I (Marcus) learned how to skeet shoot with my team. It was an excellent opportunity for those with strength to help those (like me) who had never done it before.

The maturity workouts in this book are great for group practice and can give your identity group a place to start working together as you help each other grow in maturity and strength.

CHAPTER 6

Return to Joy

JOY IS NOT A COMMON TOPIC in leadership—but it should be. Many leaders are results-oriented, bottom-line thinkers who don't see the need for sappy emotions like joy. But there is nothing sappy about joy. It is the fuel on which our brains were meant to run. In a sense, we all either run on the relational fuel of joy or on the non-relational fuel of fear. If we experience victory and only feel relief, we are running on the fuel of fear. If we love coming to work, it is because there is joy in being with our people and satisfaction in accomplishing something of value. If we dread coming to work, it will be nearly impossible to sustain long-term success.

As a motivator, fear is only meant to give us energy in short bursts. We can't run our lives or our businesses on it. Joy, on the other hand, is a motivator that never gets old. We never complain that life has too much joy! To be clear, we are talking about relational joy, not merely pleasure. Pleasure doesn't require relational attachment. It also doesn't create maturity. Addictions are generally pleasurable, but that doesn't mean they grow us into better people. On the other hand, relational joy can sustain us through all sorts of hardships and give us a reason to live.

Joy is our natural state. We feel the most like ourselves when we are experiencing relational joy. Because of this, it is very important for leaders to learn how to "return to joy" when negative emotions threaten to shut down the fast track. When emotions like shame, anger, fear, and despair dim our relational circuits, it not only affects the way we feel, it affects our performance. We aren't as creative, clear-headed, or logical when our relational circuits are struggling.

Leaders don't just need to be good at returning to joy for their own sakes. Effective leaders recognize the emotional state of their team (or individuals on the team) and help them return to joy as well. This ability to "read" people and offer needed encouragement is one of the Skills and Habits that needs to be developed so that it happens without thinking about it. It is a key factor in distinguishing mature leaders from sandbox leaders.

THE "VCR" FORMULA

There are two key elements to the process of returning to joy: validation and comfort. We can think of it as VCR, or the formula V+C=R—Validation + Comfort = Return to joy. Validating emotions is simply naming an emotion accurately and correctly identifying how big it is. This is a fast-track skill. It is part of reading people well. The fast track senses how a person is feeling—cautious, anxious, happy, embarrassed— and meets the person in that emotion. You don't need to agree that someone should be feeling the way they do. You need to acknowledge what they are actually feeling.

I (Marcus) often start meetings with a quick check in to see how people are feeling. This isn't therapy. People get one minute to say, "I'm having a great day and feeling really productive," or "I've had problems at home and I'm a little distracted," or "I'm feeling kind of nervous about the deadline for this project." The only reaction to these check-in statements is to validate the emotion with a statement like, "That sounds like it would create some anxiety, but we are glad you are here," or "You have a lot on your plate, I can see how that could get tiring," or "It sounds like we are all excited and ready to get to work." We never stop to try to solve someone's problems; we just let them know that we see where they are at and are glad to be with them.

Practicing check-ins for just a few weeks did wonders for building team chemistry. We have had team members struggle with rebellious kids, lose a house to fire, go through a divorce, as well as some less dramatic hardships. It was helpful for the team to know what they were going through, and it was helpful to the people with problems to know others were aware and respectful of their situation.

In private meetings, leaders often have to deal with the emotions of their group members. Remembering to validate emotions before fixing problems is an important element of mature leadership. This means we must name the emotion accurately, but it also means we must get the size of the feeling fairly accurately without agreeing that it should be that size. If one of our sales team seems slightly hesitant and we say, "You look like you are scared spitless," it will earn us a dirty look at best. You are overstating her feeling. If we say, "We all can get a little nervous moving forward after being turned down," we will probably get a small smile—a trace of joy. Accurate observation and validation make a person feel seen and understood.

> Remembering to validate emotions before fixing problems is an important element of mature leadership.

Comforting may sound a bit odd—like something you would expect from a mother or a therapist—but comforting is about making problems smaller. Negative emotions are usually created by the sense that we have a problem that is pushing us to or past the limits of our capacity. The longer we live on the edge of our emotional capacity, the more drained we get. If we live beyond our emotional capacity for too long, we can have a nervous breakdown.

HOW TO MAKE A PROBLEM SMALLER

Making problems smaller is comforting because it makes us feel like our situation is manageable. Sometimes we do this for ourselves, and sometimes we do it for our team or a member of our team. For example, I (Marcus) just sent an email to one of my leadership executives who had several large projects thrust her way recently. She was clearly overwhelmed, so to make her problem smaller and more manageable, I told her which project I needed her to focus on and not to worry about the others until that one was finished. I added that I didn't want her getting burned out or overwhelmed because I wanted her around and contributing for a long time.

There are times when we can't make problems smaller, but if we constantly push people past their capacity it means we are treating everything like a crisis and driving people with fear.

Here are three practices that can help make problems smaller.

1. **State what *isn't* going to happen.**

   "You're not losing your job—I just need to see improvement in this area."

   "The company had a bad month, but it doesn't mean we're going under."

   "I know some of your coworkers are difficult, but that doesn't mean the project is doomed."

2. **Find a new perspective.** One of the reasons we go to people for advice is to get new perspectives that help us look at our problems from a different angle. Sometimes people just need hope that there is a perspective that will make the situation more manageable.

3. **Make a new plan.** Sometimes problems are big because we are tackling more at one time than we can handle. Forming a new plan with more manageable steps is a great way to make problems smaller.

The more we practice VCR with ourselves, the better we get at bouncing back from difficult emotions. The more we practice it with our team, the more trust and engagement we create. Let's look at a few common emotions leaders face and what the VCR process of returning to joy might look like in each case.

FEAR AND ANXIETY

Fear is an involuntary reaction to danger. It happens in the fast track when the "flight" response gets triggered in the amygdala (assessment center). Anxiety, on the other hand, is driven by activity in the slow track. It is a reaction to imagined danger. As leaders, we all deal with fear and anxiety because there are real dangers we must face and endless scenarios that can end badly. It often doesn't take much imagination to see danger ahead and begin to feel fear.

When dealing with our own fear, the VCR process starts with validating our own emotion by acknowledging what we are feeling and how big it is. If our fear or anxiety is mild or moderate, we can often recover by taking a few deep breaths and going through the following exercise.

1. What is the worst thing that could happen?
2. What is the best thing that could happen?
3. What is the most likely thing to happen?
4. Make a plan based on what is most likely to happen.

When our fear is pushing us beyond our capacity to handle problems well, we need our people to help us. This is a time for reaching out to others in our identity group, so we don't feel all alone in our struggles.

VCR is also a helpful model when we are in the position of needing to help someone else deal with their fear or anxiety. We start by validating their emotion, and then helping them develop a plan for moving forward.

On my (Jim's) second day as an intern in a community counseling center, I was assigned to meet with the wife of a jealous man. Barely an hour after the appointment, her husband called to say he was coming at noon. He had a gun and he was going to shoot and kill me. This was no idle threat; a short time later another counselor in the area was gunned down in a parking lot by a client. I had no experience with a situation like this. I turned to my supervisor for direction, but he announced it was lunchtime and left. Rather than showing mature leadership, he played the possum and abandoned me on my second day of work! A mature leader would have taken the time to acknowledge the fear of a young intern and help him think through a plan. Instead, I was left on my own and experienced a fast-track crash. My joy elevator shut down. As a result, my slow track—where anxiety comes from—was left to pick up the pieces without any guidance from my identity center on how it was like me and my people to act in a situation like this. In minutes, I went home. My internship had gone from "highly desirable" to "I never want to go back" because the leader lacked the maturity to lead when things got hard.

Not only does this story remind us of the importance of leadership in high-stress situations, it is a good illustration of a fast-track crash. This was an extreme case. However, most crashes happen when we drift into fatigue. As stressors drain our joy, one thing too many makes our fast track cramp up. Our CASHCoW is lost. Our Conscious Attention (CA) gets focused on irritants because our Skills and Habits (SH) have been overwhelmed. In this state, we withdraw or use too much force (often anger) on others, thus damaging our ability to engage in Collaborative Work (CoW). We burn through relational capital for temporary results. In our state of being overwhelmed, we temporarily fail to see creative and cooperative solutions. This kind of brain lockup is not uncommon and a reminder of why RARE habits are so important.

DISGUST

Disgust is the feeling that wants to get away from something toxic or revolting. It is a low-energy emotion related to vomiting. Leaders often find themselves battling disgust when dealing with people who are incompetent or immature. We even see disgust between generations as millennials make "boomer jokes" and boomers shake their heads at millennials.

Leaders will often feel disgust for people with low standards and poor skills, but it is important to return to joy before engaging relationally with people. We need to check ourselves and make sure we are acting like ourselves so we can remain relational as we interact with people who have triggered disgust.

ANGER

Anger is the feeling that wants to stop injustice and pain. It is a high-energy emotion that can pump our body full of adrenaline. Most leaders feel anger particularly when their goals get blocked. When you have a plan and deadlines to meet and a coworker or supervisor does something to undermine your progress, it is easy to feel angry. If we don't return to joy from our anger, we often act in ways we later regret.

A friend of mine (Marcus) had a seasonal job with an accountant to help during tax season. This accountant was normally a very outgoing, friendly person, which was one of the reasons she took the position. But under the stress of deadlines and the weight of his workload, the man got angry a lot. He didn't know how to return to joy from his anger, and it led to some really stupid decisions. In one case, my friend had been given a large printing project. It required thousands of sheets of paper and a rather complicated process involving a very expensive printer. In the middle of this project, the accountant ran out of his office with a piece of paper in his hand, hit the stop button without asking for help, and tried to make a copy of his paper. He messed up the whole project and his paper didn't print. So he did the logical thing. He started kicking his very expensive copy machine as my friend watched, afraid to tell him that if he had waited just one minute, she could have stopped the process properly and made the copy for him, which is what he had hired her to do. Instead, his anger got the best of him and he stopped handling himself like an adult and started acting like a child. My friend experienced many moments of this type of "sandbox leadership."

A high-performing employee with a large corporation had to go into a meeting with several people who had made him really angry. However, this man had learned some skills from me (Jim) for handling anger. Before going to the meeting, he went into the bathroom and let his anger build by flaring his nostrils, clenching his fists, and wringing a towel (as mentioned in a previous exercise). The anger peaked and he was able to quiet himself with some deep breathing. He then paused to remember something he could authentically appreciate about the people in the meeting and was able to return to joy so that his relational circuits were on when he entered the room. Knowing how to return to joy from anger enabled him to act like himself and remain relational.

SHAME

Shame is the emotion we feel when someone isn't happy to be with us. It makes us want to hang our heads and hide.

If we never learn how to act like ourselves when we feel this emotion, we will become experts at avoiding it. While avoiding shame may sound like a good idea, it can lead to some disastrous consequences.

The easiest way to avoid shame is to earn your black belt in **self-justification.** People who can't act like themselves when they feel shame learn early in life to deflect shame to others. Their motto seems to be, "If one of us is going down, it isn't going to be me." Self-justification is the opposite of ownership. It is blaming others—throwing them under the bus—so we don't have to own the fact that something we did made them unhappy.

The need to avoid shame can turn people into predators. Their brains go into enemy mode. One minute they can be your best friend, but let shame get triggered and they can turn on you in a heartbeat. They suddenly see you as an enemy to be defeated. This sudden shift between friend mode and enemy mode often catches us off guard. It is easy to think, "I like this person when they are happy, and I don't like them when they are scary, so I'll do what I can to keep them happy." It is not uncommon for the group surrounding a leader who lacks the ability to handle shame, to tiptoe around sensitive issues that cause eruptions. Without realizing it, the entire group begins to police each other, making sure that no one triggers the leader. Instead of the group helping the leader learn a healthy way to handle shame, they all live in fear of triggering enemy mode.

The technical term for an inability to return to joy from shame is narcissism. One of the reasons it is so hard to help narcissists is their self-justification skill. Narcissists have convinced themselves they are whoever they think they need to be to avoid pain and survive. I (Jim) wrote a book on narcissism titled *The Pandora Problem.* I observed that narcissistic leaders find, gather, or produce groups of possums who will perform to avoid the narcissist's enemy mode. But rather than sending the narcissist into therapy, the "support group" around the narcissist can change. By learning to keep relationships bigger than problems, the group begins acting like themselves instead of turning into possums. Groups are sometimes capable of acting like good leaders to themselves, but how much better when the leader is helping the group. Don't be fooled and think that the narcissist in the room is always the boss! Consider who makes you think, "If I say anything, it will only make things worse." Many a boss and supervisor has tiptoed around a narcissist. It is a RARE leader who hasn't.

> Don't be fooled and think the narcissist in the room is always the boss!

MATURITY WORKOUT: PLANNING

Every leader deals with anxiety at times, because we can all imagine scenarios that can get pretty scary. We start to ask ourselves questions like, "What if I blow this deadline?" "What if the manager gets angry?" "What if the economy tanks?'

The next time you feel anxiety, try this exercise.

1. Quiet with the BEST practices we learned in chapter 1 (or at least a few deep breaths).

2. Ask yourself, "What is the worst thing that could happen?" Write it out.

3. Ask yourself, "What is the best thing that could happen?" Write that out.

4. Ask yourself, "What is the most likely thing to happen?" Make a plan based on that.

5. Share that plan with someone else and ask for feedback.

6. Take a second to thank your listener. You will probably get a smile that helps you return to joy.

As you make your plan, state your goals, list the resources at your disposal, and identify some steps you can take to start moving toward your goals. The simple process of having a plan can be a helpful way to reduce stress and begin to return to joy.

CHAPTER 7

Endure Hardship Well

WHEN A WORLDWIDE PANDEMIC combined with political and social divisions at unprecedented levels swept across the globe in 2020, it changed the playing field for most leaders in a hurry. We were suddenly confronted with unique and often-overwhelming problems and few proven pathways on which to travel. In addition to the new challenges involved in keeping businesses open and developing new strategies on the fly, we had to deal with hard emotions. Many of us felt anxiety if not outright panic. Many of our coworkers, employees, clients, and family members were angry, scared, and overwhelmed. Situations like this cry out for mature leaders who can handle the emotion of the moment as well as the practical strategy challenges it creates.

The great leaders of history are often held in high regard specifically because of their ability to navigate the hard times they faced. We admire people like Abraham Lincoln, Winston Churchill, and Nelson Mandela because of their ability to endure hardship well and call people to a greater vision.

Mandela famously endured twenty-seven years in prison for his political activism. When he was released, many expected to see an angry, vengeful man. Instead, he won the world over by preaching unity and peace. The ability to suffer well has been a hallmark of many great leaders who combined a resolute vision and relational maturity.

Sandbox leaders handle hardship like children. A particular bank manager comes to mind. He was a very immature man with many addictions and eccentricities who was given to tantrums, meltdowns, and mood swings. He was the branch manager of a financial firm. He had been with the company a long time and an effective salesperson. However, he lacked the maturity to lead effectively. His executive assistant seemed to double as the man's mother. Her unwritten job description was to keep everything running smoothly so that nothing upset him. Eventually, the board of directors figured out what was going on and made some changes. To everyone's delight they made the executive assistant the new president—she seemed to be running everything anyway. It was a good decision. Her maturity transformed a toxic environment into a place people loved to work.

The immaturity of this manager was clearly demonstrated by his inability to act like himself when he got upset. When things got hard, people walked on eggshells around him, never sure which leader they would get—angry, avoidant, and anxious, or charming and friendly. Needless to say, his inability to act like himself under pressure did not generate trust or engagement in the people he led. It certainly did not create a joyful atmosphere in the workplace.

No one is born with maturity. It is something that must be earned and there are no shortcuts. Neither is maturity simply a choice you make. It is a capacity we develop over time that requires the help of others. Unfortunately, most of us lag far behind the optimum level of maturity for our age. We may bear the weight of being leaders, but most of us missed out on significant elements of the maturation process. As a result, we find ourselves underdeveloped for our age, and carrying more weight than we know how to handle.

TRAUMA AND MATURITY

Missing out on the preparation we were supposed to get from older family members is traumatizing to our development. Just as a plant will be traumatized (and possibly die) if it does not get enough water, the right kind of soil, or the right balance of sunlight, so our maturity development suffers when we don't get the nurture and training we need from parents and extended family.

The hole left when we miss something important in our upbringing is called Trauma A. The "A" stands for "Absence." We all experience trauma in our lives because of the absence of good stuff we needed in order to grow. The impact of what we miss can be catastrophic to our maturity. The only solution for the holes created by Trauma A is to learn the missing skills later in life. This will not be as easy as learning the skills when we were young. But there is no other path forward. Just as it is harder to learn French or learn how to play an instrument at an older age, so the task will take more focused work than when we were young, but it can be done, and we will need help.

In addition to Trauma A, many of us also have Trauma B in our past. Trauma B refers to the "bad" stuff that happen to us, such as verbal, physical, psychological, and sexual abuse. Bad experiences stunt maturity by causing a person to live in fear. Fear is the toxic alternative to joy, and it thrives when maturity development gets stalled. While Trauma B can—and often does—stunt maturity development, Trauma A will ALWAYS stunt our maturity development.

MATURITY HOLES

When families, churches, and communities do not know the required tasks for growing maturity or supply the essential care that prepares people for the next stage of life, the inevitable result will be holes in our maturity skills. These holes in our maturity lead to all sorts of problems. Here are some of the most common results.

- **Avoidance.** When we don't learn how to endure hardship well, we develop an avoidant lifestyle. We avoid hard tasks, hard relationships, and hard emotions. The more situations we feel driven to avoid, the smaller our world gets. We often fill our world with entertainment or become "workaholics" in order to avoid stress at home.

- **Addiction.** Holes in our maturity nearly always end in some form of addiction, and generally multiple addictions to a variety of substances and experiences. Addiction is a clear sign there are holes in our maturity that need to be filled.

- **Anxiety.** Underdeveloped maturity makes it much easier to feel anxious about life. A lower capacity level means it takes less to make us feel overwhelmed, and overwhelmed emotions tend to create fear and anxiety about the future.

- **Anger.** A short fuse is another clear sign that there are holes in our maturity development. Some people say, "I'm just an angry person, you'd better get used to it." But this is simply justifying a lack of maturity development. Learning how to return to joy from anger is an important maturity skill.

Sadly, we live in a culture that is experiencing a maturity crisis. It is hard to find fully formed adults who act like adults. It is even harder to find parent- and elder-level adults who are good at forming character in the next generation. We need a generation of leaders to rise up and begin changing the maturity level of the culture. Imagine a world in which people were able to remain relational and acted like themselves

> Imagine a world where people were able to remain relational when they disagreed about politics.

when they disagreed about politics. Imagine what would happen to our families if more parents had fully formed habits that made it easy to pass on relational skills to the next generation. How would greater maturity change the workplace, the government, our families, even the church? It would be truly revolutionary.

SIX STAGES OF MATURITY

The Life Model[1] identifies six stages in the maturity development process that span conception to death. The six stages are:

- In utero
- Infants
- Children
- Adults
- Parents
- Elders

Let's start with a few observations about these stages.

1. Maturity looks different at each stage of development. An infant who reaches maturity for her age is ready to move to the next one. A child who develops the maturity skills appropriate to his/her age is ready to become an adult. We don't have time for a complete explanation of the maturity development process, but this chapter will include an introduction to the kind of skills that need to be developed at each stage and what happens if they don't.

2. There is no adolescent stage. Adolescence, as we know it to-day, is a modern contrivance. Biologically, people become adults when they pass through puberty. Theoretically, these young adults could become parents pretty quickly if they weren't careful. Adolescence was invented largely during the Industrial Revolution to delay young people entering the workforce, and then continued because so many people entered their teen years unprepared to be adults. Learning how to be an adult among adults is a crucial stage of life that we should master long before we get married and have children of our own.

3. Moving from stage to stage always involves a form of death and rebirth. The fetus in the womb must abandon the comforts of complete dependence on mother in order to be born. The infant must "die to" being completely dependent in order to enter the childhood stage and begin learning how to take care of himself. The child must "die to" being only responsible for one in order to embrace the adult task of learning to take care of two or more people at the same time. We "die to" the relative ease of the adult years with the birth of our first child. When our youngest child becomes an adult, we "die to" the parenting stage of life in order to be reborn into our elder years. Those who successfully let go of one stage and move on to the next continue to mature. Those who do not make that transition successfully find themselves stuck. While our comments about dying to each stage are metaphors, a process called apoptosis actually does kill and remove elements in the brain at the end of the infant and child stage. The brain needs to learn new functions at the start of each stage of maturity.

4. Our maturity development gets stunted when no one walks us through the process of preparing for the next stage of life, helping us say goodbye to the former stage and welcoming us into the next. Successful transitions require community. Coaching transitions is one of the tasks of our identity group and one of the reasons multi-generational family is such a powerful force in maturity development.

Let's take a brief look at the five maturity stages from birth to elder and how unresolved trauma can leave us with yawning gaps in our ability to provide RARE leadership.

The Infant Stage. We will use the word infancy to include both the baby and toddler years. Infants need lots of smiles to build a solid, joyful resilience for life. Babies who don't get a lot of relational attention don't fully develop the parts of their brain that control their ability to live with joy and regulate emotion. This lack of brain development will impair them for the rest of their lives unless steps are taken to do some repair work. The good news is that the part of the brain that experiences relational joy and remembers who we are can continue to grow for as long as we live if it gets enough joy exercise.

Infants also need people to validate and comfort them, so they learn how to return to joy from upsetting emotions. The experience of being validated and comforted builds pathways in the brain that train little ones how to bounce back from hard experiences. It helps to build resilience. Adults need to guide them in learning how to return to joy so that as adults they do this without needing to think about it.

Leaders who are stuck with infant-level emotional capacity aren't there because they choose to be. They are stuck because the development process didn't go well and still needs to be completed. However, the effect of infant-level leadership on the group is not good. Like babies, infant-level leaders don't know how to ask for what they need. They expect other people to recognize what they are dealing with and take care of their needs without being asked. What these sandbox leaders are really good at is letting you know they are upset. Just like a baby fusses and whines and shrieks and cries, and the mom learns to tell what each upset sound means, so the infant-level leader expects others to figure out why he or she is upset and take care of the problem. It is not uncommon for such a leader to have an assistant who doubles as something of an emotional mother. The assistant's job is to help the leader calm down and to interpret his/her emotional outbursts for the rest of the team.

The Child Stage. During the child years (weaning through puberty) we are supposed to learn how to take care of ourselves.

We are not supposed to take care of the whole family— bad things happen to our emotional development when we have to parent our parents. However, we are supposed to be trained in all the skills we need to turn life into an adventure. Children need to learn what is satisfying and how to work hard to get what satisfies. They learn that skills require discipline. If older people help them form those disciplines, children learn how to wait for and work for what is good. Music lessons are a great way to pass on these skills, as are gardening, farming, athletics, camping, and many other activities. The goal is for children to recognize what brings their heart to life. Childhood teaches that some things bring a satisfaction that is worth the sacrifice. If children don't learn these skills, they will not develop a fully formed identity because our sense of identity is directly related to what we find satisfying.

During the child years children need to become responsible for the words used to describe their emotions. People who finish their child-level years without a strong sense of identity and without good emotional regulation skills will enter their adult years battling emotional instability.

Children who learn how to take care of themselves, recover from upsetting emotions, and try new adventures create a wonderful foundation for moving into their adult years with emotional stability and a clear sense of self.

Leaders who are stuck at the child level of maturity are generally pretty good at taking care of themselves. Unlike infant leaders, they can tell you what they need and what they want from you. However, they run into trouble dealing with the needs of others. Child-level leaders take a "me or you," "us or them" approach. They take sides and help one side at the expense of the other. If child leaders help others, they neglect themselves. Because people at child-level maturity struggle to take care of themselves, they tend to build teams that exist to make their own life easier rather than making sure they have the best team for the mission.

Sandbox leadership is a crisis because the majority of leaders are stuck at either infant- or child-level maturity. To test this theory, I (Marcus) occasionally ask people in the service industry about their managers. Whether it is a barista, a hotel clerk, or a car rental agent, I tell them I do leadership training and ask, "Would you consider your manager to be an emotionally mature person?" The most common reaction I get is laughter. Once in a while someone will say yes. And in every case that person will also say that they really like working for them.

When people laugh, I follow up by asking, "Would you say your manager is competent?" At this question, most people say yes. "So, you would say your boss is competent and knows how to do their job but lacks relational and emotional skills. Is that right?" Overwhelmingly, the answer I get is yes. This makes sense, since most managers get their jobs because they are good at getting work done, not good at dealing with people and elevated emotions. What separates the competent managers people *have to* follow from the rare managers people *love to* follow is emotional and relational maturity.

Let's look at the next three levels of maturity.

The Adult Stage. Many people think of the adult stage as starting at age 21 or possibly age 25 when the brain is generally fully developed. However, extending childhood expectations past puberty does not deal adequately with the enormous physical changes to the brain and the body that take place as we enter our teens. It also postpones important maturity development tasks. While it is common in our culture for people to be proud of the fact that they refuse to grow up and want to stay a child forever, this does not make for great leadership.

As an adult we can quiet ourselves and share joy (two infant-level skills we have mastered), we can take care of ourselves (a child-level skill we have mastered), but we are beginning to learn some new skills as well:

- We can take care of two people at the same time, whereas a child can only take care of one person— themselves.

- We learn how to drive hard bargains that are fair for both parties and create win-win solutions. Without adult maturity the only way I can win is for you to lose.

- We form a strong sense of belonging with our people. Knowing who our people are gives us a clear sense of identity. Children get their identity primarily from their parents. As adults, our primary identity is tied to who our people are.

Knowing who our people are clarifies our values. We know how it is like our people to act and what is important to us. As leaders, our primary task is to create identity groups. We want the groups we lead to know who they are, what they value, and how it is like them to act. When such an identity takes hold within the group, they police each other and encourage one another to be the best version of themselves they can be.

The Parent Stage. Parenthood is meant to follow several years of life as an adult. One of the reasons our culture has such a family crisis on its hands is that most parents have not yet successfully become adults; thus, they essentially are forced to skip a stage in the maturity process. Based on our experience, most marriages in America involve an infant-level husband and a child-level wife trying to raise kids. From this perspective, it is not hard to see why so many parents are overwhelmed.

> One of the reasons our culture has such a family crisis on its hands is that most parents have not yet successfully become adults.

In leadership terms, parent-level maturity is demonstrated when we are taking care of ourselves, working successfully with a team, and ready to start investing in others.

Parent-level maturity means we are confident in our own success and can focus on the success of those we lead. We are driven by the success of our team and growth in members of our team. Our team success is our own success.

The Elder Stage. The elder years essentially start when we become an empty nester. Our children are grown, and we have a lot of experience at dealing with the hardships of life. Our wisdom and emotional capacity have grown through the highs and lows we have navigated. Our energy may not be what it was, but we have a lot to offer. At this stage of life, elders may still lead organizations, but often they are ready for the important role of helping people fill the holes in their maturity development. Elder-level leaders lend stability and provide guidance for their people.

In our youth-oriented culture, two problems emerge. First, we discard elders because they are not as energetic, and they tend to cost more than those just starting in the workplace. However, elders contribute a great deal to the culture of an organization. Elder guidance often contributes to success and helps to avoid costly errors. A second problem is that people often try to fill the role of elder prematurely. People at the parent stage of life put their work before their family. At the stage when their children and families need investment, they put all their energy into work. It is easy to fall into this trap when workplace needs are great and people are counting on us. The needs of the many seem like they should outweigh the needs of the few. But in this context, that is not true. We don't want parents sacrificing their children on the altar of corporate success. We want parents to take care of their family first.

Understanding the stages of maturity helps us assess where we are in our own maturity development. They also identify some of the skills and habits that need to be strengthened because trauma has left holes in our development. The leaders who learn to endure hardship well are the ones who bring adult-, parent-, or elder-level skills to the table. The intangibles they offer make every team they serve better.

MATURITY WORKOUT: WELCOMING SHAME

Growing our ability to endure hardship well is largely about learning how to recover from upsetting emotions. One of the most difficult to master is returning to joy from shame. Shame is the emotion we feel when someone is not glad to be with us. We may feel this way when we get a bad review, lose a sale, or even when someone doesn't smile at us when we meet. If the feeling of shame gets interpreted as "They are not happy to see me because I am bad," it can become toxic quite easily.

The ability to act like ourselves and not be controlled by shame is an important key to effective leadership. It is also an important key to sales. The best salespeople are the ones who return to joy quickly from shame. They excel at meeting people who are not happy to be with them and transforming that encounter into a joyful connection. Top salespeople bounce back from the shame feeling of not making a sale and get on to the next opportunity. The conscious slow track may think of lost sales in lots of ways, but the fast track reaction to anyone who turns us away is a little burst of unhappiness in the brain's shame circuit.

Most of us avoid shame and deflect it to others rather than feeling it and dealing with it. One of the reasons for this is that if we have not mastered the art of feeling shame and recovering, we will treat all shame as if it is toxic. But the truth is, we cannot grow as a person without experiencing some shame. We all have weaknesses, we all have holes in our maturity, we all make mistakes and let people down at times. Learning how to deal with the emotions created by failure and disappointing others is an important skill related to enduring hardship well.

The maturity workout for this chapter is to invite healthy shame messages from others.

- **Step 1:** Invite honest critique. Ask someone you know and trust to comment on an area of weakness in your life. If they are unwilling to share a critique, it may be a sign that they fear you will be a predator who will use their participation against them.

- **Step 2:** Thank them for caring enough to be honest with you.

- **Step 3:** Assume the critique is true. Do not justify your behavior. Instead, take at least three minutes to make a list of two or three things you can do to improve in this area.

- **Step 4:** Share with the person at least one step you are taking to grow in that area and thank them again for their input.

CHAPTER 8

Putting Together a Growth Plan

WE ALL HAVE HOLES in our maturity—areas that need attention. In this chapter, we want to combine several of the insights we have covered throughout this book and help you put together a plan for personal growth.

To keep this simple, you can think of your growth plan as "Taking AIM" on the holes in your maturity development.

- **Assessment:** Take a short assessment to get an idea of where you are starting related to maturity development.
- **Identity Group:** Form an identity group that will work together on the exercises in this book.
- **Maturity Workouts:** As a group, do the maturity workouts in this book together.

HOW MATURE AM I?

You may have read about the five levels of maturity in the last chapter and thought to yourself, "How can I know what level of maturity I am at?" Here is a simple assessment tool to help you get started in answering that question. The goal of this tool is not to define you or insult you, but to give you a sense of where you need to start, and which skills might need your most immediate attention.

Infant

A lack of security, smiles, and/or emotional synchronization can leave us stuck in infant-level maturity. Much of the American population is stuck here. To start your assessment, answer the following questions.

1. Do I blow up easily and expect others to change their behavior simply because I am upset?
2. Do I expect others to anticipate my needs and act without being asked?
3. Do I pout easily and sulk when I don't get my way?
4. Do I get stuck in negative emotions for days at a time with no idea of how to recover?

If the answer to any of these questions is yes, it means you have a hole in your maturity at the infant level that needs to be addressed. This means you need to focus especially on the skills of quieting and appreciation.

Child

If we did not develop a secure identity and learn how to work hard and wait for what is satisfying, we may be stuck at child-level maturity. Respond to the following questions to do a short self-evaluation.

1. Am I good at getting my own tasks done, but don't like to be bothered by the needs of others?
2. Do I tell others what to do, as opposed to working creatively and collaboratively together?
3. Do I avoid learning new skills because it feels intimidating?
4. Do I think in terms of what is best for me as opposed to what is best for my group?
5. Do I own my mistakes or blame others when I fall short?

If you answer yes to any of the first three questions, you have a hole in your maturity at the child level. This means focusing on CAKE and VCR skills is likely a good place to start.

Adult

The adult years are about forming a strong group identity in which I know who my people are and actively work for the good of the group. How would you answer these questions?

1. Do I actively seek win/win solutions?
2. Do I try to solve problems collaboratively or wish others would leave me alone to solve the problems myself?
3. Do I create belonging with others who become my people?
4. Is it like me to take the good of the team into consideration?

If the answer is yes to these questions, it means you have

developed the capacity to function at an adult level. If the answer is no, there are holes that need to be filled. Working in an identity group and developing a collective sense of "who we are" might be a good place to focus.

Parent

Parents are life-givers. They sacrificially give of themselves to make sure that their children develop the skills needed to reach their potential. While raising a family is the most intense way to reach parent maturity, there are other ways. Parent maturity looks at weakness and immaturity as a place to help others grow and make us all more joyful. Ask yourself . . .

1. Do I have a family of my own that needs me to be engaged because my kids are not yet adults?
2. Am I careful not to let my work rob me of family time, since this is the only window I have for raising my children?
3. Do I love creating a life-giving culture at work in which people regularly grow skills and enjoy being together?

Parenting is primarily about our families. One of the most important aspects of living with parent-level maturity is to understand the priority that family needs to have during this season of life. Bringing parent-level maturity to the workplace means you can get your own work done but enjoy forming teams that work collaboratively as well.

Elder

Elders are essentially empty nesters who are done raising their kids. They may have adult children living at home, but they have successfully navigated the first four stages of maturity and have the earned maturity to fill holes, create a sense of family, and carry weight well because they have spent so many years enduring hardship well, first as adults and then as parents.

1. Are my kids grown? If so, I am a candidate for the elder stage of life.
2. Rather than take my identity from the achievements and success of my children, I have learned to be content, even if they go a different direction with their lives.
3. I regularly notice people in the workplace who are struggling and find ways to step in and provide mentoring.
4. Others seek my wisdom and rely on me to carry the weight of problems that arise. I find this trust more meaningful than burdensome.

Once you have worked through the questions in this assessment, it is a good idea to start focusing on the issues related to the lowest level of maturity first. Identifying growth areas can make the maturity workouts you do in your identity groups more effective.

IDENTITY GROUP

An identity group is a place where you can reveal your weaknesses, knowing people are there to help each other grow. It is a place to practice skills, discuss life, and form relationships with people who help you handle the weight of life. This group isn't normally the team you lead or a group of coworkers. It is often a group you assemble via the internet from all over the world. However, it is ideal to have a group that can meet in person at least annually, so that when you connect virtually, you have some relational history on which to build.

The maturity workout in chapter 5 explains how to get a group started. Here is a quick review.

- Form a group.
- Create an identity statement. For example, 'We are rare leaders who . . . " or "We are protector leaders who practice the four S's":
  + Stories (learn each other's story)
  + Service (serve together to become a force for good)
  + Study (select material related to growth to discuss)
  + Socialize (spend time together in social settings, especially those that involve skill development)
- Finally, use the Maturity Workouts to focus your attention on new habits you are seeking to build.

Without an identity group, the odds that you will actually develop the habits that fill the holes in your maturity virtually disappear. Self-effort, isolation, and hiddenness work against maturity development because maturity is anchored in relational competence. There are some skills you can work on before an identity group is in place, but the group will serve as a catalyst for change far more powerful than self-discipline.

MATURITY WORKOUTS

The maturity workouts found throughout this book give you a concrete way to start building rare habits into your life. Many of these can be done independently of an identity group (especially quieting, appreciating, and some of the other practices), but all of them will take on a greater transformational power if combined with an identity group experience.

Not only is it a good idea to use these workouts for your own personal development, but they can also be easily adapted into a form of staff training to help grow a relationally and emotionally healthy culture for your team.

Here is a quick review of the workouts in the book:

- Quieting
- Appreciating others
- Appreciation
- Curiosity
- Planning
- Welcoming shame
- Ending self-justification

At the organization I (Marcus) lead, we like to hire people who have already been through this type of skill training, but for those who have not, we try to get them up to speed as quickly as possible because we believe maturity and joy are foundational to creativity, problem solving, and sustainability.

One person, who worked for us in a part-time capacity before taking a full-time position with another organization referred to her experience as "healing." She came in feeling beaten down, used, and burned out. She left feeling like her old self and ready to tackle a major new initiative at her new company. Our goal is to create a work environment that people don't want to leave because we are accomplishing meaningful work in a relational way that keeps joy high. When they do leave, we want them to take what they have experienced and spread it to other organizations.

MATURITY MAKES THINGS BETTER

We need more mature leaders. We need them in the workplace, in the halls of government, in our educational institutions, in our families, our religious communities, and in our day-to-day lives. Wherever you are and whatever you do, maturity makes things better. Intentionally working with a group to build the skills and habits practiced by rare leaders will do more than make you more effective in the workplace. It will impact your family life too. Many people who have gone through this material have commented that as much help as they got for their work environment, they saw even more fruit in their home life.

We encourage you not simply to read this book, but to take AIM at your own maturity. Assess where you are at. Initiate an identity group. Make time for the maturity workouts. Give it three months, then retake the assessment and take stock of the improvement you see in your relationships and your workplace environment. If you are seeing progress and like the direction things are going, take it to the next level and incorporate RARE training into the fabric of your culture. Imagine what becomes possible with increased trust, joy, and engagement in the people you lead.

MATURITY WORKOUT—
ENDING SELF-JUSTIFICATION

One of the most common habits of immature and narcissistic leaders is self-justification. If we are going to endure hardship well by remaining relational, acting like ourselves, and returning to joy, we need to train ourselves to avoid self-justification. When we don't handle shame well, we tend to hear all shame messages as **toxic** shame messages. This generally creates a defensive reaction that seeks to condemn someone else. Condemning others in order to justify themselves is the biggest club narcissists carry.

Maturity, on the other hand, requires us to be able to experience shame without going into enemy mode. We need to learn how to remain relational and act like ourselves instead of turning into someone much more predatory. One way to grow our capacity to handle shame with maturity is to intentionally invite shame messages from others and respond to those messages with appreciation.

Take time this week to track how often you defend yourself from attack (or perceived attack) with self-justification that includes blaming or condemning someone else. Record this in writing (possibly a journal):

1. Who attacked?

2. What was the attack?

3. How did it make me feel?

4. How did I justify myself?

5. How could I have taken more ownership?

6. What would maturity look like in this situation?

Track a few of these situations and discuss them with your identity group.

Acknowledgments

I (Marcus) am grateful to the many leaders who both challenged concepts in this writing to make them clearer and who told stories of how this material had changed their lives. I also want to acknowledge the support of my family and the editorial team of Duane Sherman and Betsey Newenhuyse for their insight and direction as we completed this project. It is always a pleasure to be able to work with Jim Wilder. He has a unique way of challenging conventional thought and pushing people to attempt just a little bit more than they thought they could do.

I (Jim) am very aware that the ideas and experience I bring to life, work, and this book are the result of participating in an active and determined group identity. By keeping company and pushing the limits of our knowledge and experience, we have found practical uses for ethical brain science. For example, I began by working with Marcus's professor father, and when the next generation of Dr. Warners came along we continued building together. Dr. Allan Schore, Dr. Daniel Siegal, Dr. Giulio Tononi, Dr. Iian McGilchrist, Dr. Karl Lehman, Dr. Antonio Damasio, and Dr. Edward Lee Travis have contributed their teaching into a pool of real-world experimenters I call my friends. Thanks to Marcus and Duane Sherman for seeing the market for brain science applied to enterprise.

Notes

Introduction

1. Visit lifemodel.org for more material and free downloads on this approach to maturity.

Chapter 1: Leaders We Love to Follow

1. Richard Davis, "We Need More Mature Leaders," *Harvard Business Review*, October 18, 2011. Richard Davis, PhD, is CEO of Kilberry Leadership Advisors, a firm of management psychologists that provides executive assessment and development services to some of North America's most prominent leaders. He is also author of *The Intangibles of Leadership*.

2. Ibid.

3. Margaret Heffernan, "Forget the Pecking Order at Work," TED.com, May 2015, https://www.ted.com/talks/margaret_heffernan_forget_the_pecking_order_at_work.

4. "Denmark Has the Best Work-Life Balance in Europe," Study in Denmark, http://studyindenmark.dk/news/denmark-has-the-best-work-life-balance-in-europe. According to both the 2013 and 2016 World Happiness Report, Denmark was the world's happiest country; Oliver Smith, "Denmark Regains Title of 'World's Happiest Country,'" March 16, 2016, https:// www.telegraph.co.uk/travel/news/denmark-regains-title-of-happiest-country/.

5. We say this because infants younger than eighteen months of age handle every new emotion as if they are a different person. They need adults in their world to meet them in these emotions and help them learn how to act like themselves regardless of how they feel. Babies only learn how to regulate their emotions and recover with help from others. If they don't get that help, they will grow into children and eventually into adults who still function like infants when certain emotions get triggered.

6. "R.A.R.E. Leadership with Chad Krober," Justin Stoddard, YouTube video, October 5, 2019, https://www.youtube.com/watch?v=-LFjyPvlVtg.

7. Marcus Warner and Stefanie Hinman, *Building Bounce: How to Grow Emotional Resilience* (Carmel, IN: Deeper Walk International, 2020), 73–76.

Chapter 2: The Brain Science Behind Maturity

1. For an excellent review of the differing functions of the left and right hemispheres of the brain, watch the TED Talk presentation by Iain McGilchrist, "The Divided Brain," October 2011, https://www.ted.com/talks/iain_mcgilchrist_the_divided_brain.

2. Social intelligence is a broader concept than EQ or emotional intelligence. It includes EQ but goes beyond that to include our competence at engaging within the social systems of our world.

Chapter 3: Mature Leadership in Practice

1. The description of this nursing unit was inspired by material found in Dr. Paul White's book, *The Vibrant Workplace: Overcoming the Obstacles to Building a Culture of Appreciation* (Chicago: Northfield, 2017).

2. Zach Lenz, "Swinney Found Joy in the Moment—Not the Accomplishment," *Sports Illustrated*, April 16, 2019, https://www.si.com/college/clemson/football/swinney-found-joy-in-the-moment-not-the-accomplish.

Chapter 7: Endure Hardship Well

1. The Life Model is an idealized paradigm of how maturity development is supposed to happen at each stage of life. It was developed by Jim Wilder and the team at Shepherd's House in Southern California.

About the Authors

Dr. Jim Wilder is a clinical psychologist, author, and international speaker who develops ways to apply brain science to the ways we live and work. Wilder has trained leaders on five continents for thirty years both learning and teaching resilience in the Netherlands, Southern Sudan, India, Bhutan, Sri Lanka, Eastern Europe, Mexico, Korea, Thailand, Chile, Brazil, and Canada. Wilder is the thinker behind the Life Model, a lifespan guide to being fully human. He is the author of numerous books and articles (now in thirteen languages) focused on maturity and relational skills.

Dr. Marcus Warner is the author of over a dozen books related to relationships and emotional resilience including the co-authored books *Building Bounce: How to Grow Emotional Resilience*, *The 4 Habits of Joy-Filled Marriages*, and *The 4 Habits of Raising Joy-Filled Kids*. He has taught corporate and nonprofit groups on four continents and runs a Christian nonprofit organization that focuses on helping people grow personal maturity.

You appreciate your coworkers—
but do they feel your appreciation?

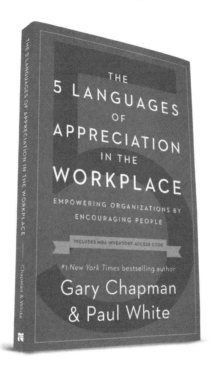

Overcome the fear of speaking truth
by learning to do it with love.

In a society where sensitivities take precedence
over truth, it can often feel impossible to openly
speak your mind. In *Candor*, you'll learn how
combining truth and love leads to more effective
leadership and healthier relationships—even in a
day and age when many remain silent for fear of
speaking up.

978-0-8024-2077-0 | also available as eBook and audiobook

What separates happy marriages from miserable ones?

These authors have studied relationships (and neuroscience) and discovered four habits that keep your joy switch turned on and your fear factors turned off. Retrain your brain to make joy your default setting by practicing the 15-minute exercises at the end of each chapter. When you experience joy regularly, problems feel manageable, and your marriage stays strong.

978-0-8024-1907-1 | also available as eBook and audiobook

How do kids move from being fear-filled to joy-filled?

Marcus Warner *and* Chris Coursey

The 4 Habits of Raising *Joy-Filled* Kids

*A Simple Model for Developing
Your Child's Maturity—at Every Stage*

NORTHFIELD
PUBLISHING

Raising kids to become happy, confident, and productive adults is doable—not just by super-parents, but by anyone willing to apply some key principles. The authors help you learn to make parenting decisions that bring joy to yourself—the essential first step—and then to those kids whose young lives are in your hands. You'll never regret investing in joy!

978-0-8024-2172-2 | also available as eBook and audiobook